Song of My Life

Song of My Life

A Biography of Margaret Walker

Carolyn J. Brown

UNIVERSITY PRESS OF MISSISSIPPI ✦ JACKSON

www.upress.state.ms.us

The University Press of Mississippi is a member of the Association of
American University Presses.

Copyright © 2014 by University Press of Mississippi
All rights reserved
Manufactured in the United States of America

First printing 2014

∞

Library of Congress Cataloging-in-Publication Data

Brown, Carolyn J., author.
Song of my life : a biography of Margaret Walker / Carolyn J. Brown.
pages cm
Includes bibliographical references and index.
ISBN 978-1-62846-147-3 (hardback) — ISBN 978-1-62846-148-0 (ebook)
1. Walker, Margaret, 1915–1998. 2. African American women authors—
Biography. 3. African Americans—Intellectual life—20th century. I. Title.
PS3545.A517Z56 2014
812'.52—dc23

[B]   2014017812

British Library Cataloging-in-Publication Data available

To Lus—thank you for bringing me to Mississippi

And to Carla, for showing me the way when I got here

Margaret Walker, seated in Eudora Welty's favorite reading chair, Eudora Welty's house, Jackson, Mississippi, 1998. Photograph © H. Kay Holloway.

I wonder if I can live to finish it. I keep feeling it should be the best thing I've ever done. It should be a very good work. I wonder sometimes if the beauty I feel I have experienced in my life can be beautifully expressed there. Somebody criticized me once about *Jubilee* and said my style was awful, that I didn't sound like a poet. I worried about that for a while, and then I learned afterwards that this was just malicious criticism. It didn't matter too much, because other critics said I was singing a folksong in *Jubilee*. They heard the rhythms in the work. This book about my life will not be confessional. It won't be purely social and intellectual history. But I do want it to be a song of my life.

Margaret Walker

Contents

10. Final Years
Awards, Recognitions, and Unfinished Work 88

Author's Note

⊂⊃

In 1998, in an advertisement for a film documentary about Margaret Walker, Nikki Giovanni, world-renowned poet, educator, activist, and close personal friend of Margaret Walker, described Walker as "the most famous person nobody knows." I have to confess I was one of those people—I had never heard of Walker through four years of college and six years of graduate school, and even after more than twenty years of academic teaching, reading, and writing. It was not until I moved to Jackson, Mississippi, and I was reading an article in the January 2012 edition of *Southern Living* magazine entitled "Mississippi's Literary Trail" that I first came across the name Margaret Walker.

I remember the moment exactly. I had just completed my book about Eudora Welty, *A Daring Life: A Biography of Eudora Welty*, and was contemplating what to write next. I was excited to see the article in *Southern Living* because I knew it would mention the Eudora Welty House, a place near and dear to my heart as I had spent many hours there researching my book. However, after the section of the article devoted to the Welty House, the story continued and said to be sure to also visit "the Margaret Walker Center, home to the nation's second largest collection of a modern black female author's papers (second only to Maya Angelou's)." I was stunned. Who was Margaret Walker? And, why, as well read as I professed to be, did I know nothing about her?

I rushed to my *Norton Anthology of Literature by Women*, my trusted source for the most complete collection of women writers, and saw that she was indeed included. I then quickly looked for information about her online, and discovered there was no book biography about her. As I collected more and more bits and pieces online about this fascinating woman, I realized that I had found my next book subject—a second important woman writer from Jackson who had been sorely overlooked yet had had friendships with many of our most well-known twentieth-century African American writers, such as Langston Hughes, Richard Wright, Ralph Ellison, Alice Walker, Nikki Giovanni, and Sonia Sanchez.

My second important discovery happened upon my first visit to the Margaret Walker Center at Jackson State University. Archivist Angela Stewart showed me Margaret Walker's unpublished autobiography: pages and pages of her life story that had recently been digitized and was available online. Walker had hoped to share her story with the world, but poor health prevented her from finishing several books she had hoped to complete at the end of her life—her autobiography was one of those unfinished projects.

Angela Stewart and Dr. Robert Luckett, director of the center, also recommended I contact Dr. Maryemma Graham at the University of Kansas, as she was the preeminent Walker scholar and was herself working on a biography of Walker. I contacted Dr. Graham right away, and she was extremely supportive of my book project: a shorter, more concise introduction to the life of Walker, targeting middle-school and high-school-age students as well as the general reader. Dr. Graham is currently writing the scholarly, definitive biography of Walker to be published by Oxford, and was generous with her time and support of my book.

Margaret Walker's unpublished autobiography provided me with the raw material I needed to write my book; however, I soon discovered while reading it that she repeats herself often and tells many versions of the same events and stories. The versions are never drastically different; she may add a detail in one version that is missing in another. She also gave many interviews late in her life, collected in *Conversations with Margaret Walker* (edited by Dr. Maryemma Graham), that include versions of these same events and provide additional details and biographical information. As a biographer, I sorted through all these different versions. It has been my intent to tell Margaret Walker's story the way she would have wanted and as much as possible in her voice; hence, a plethora of quotes are included. I also have quoted lines from her poems and excerpts from her essays where they apply. Truly, no one says it better than Margaret.

It is my hope that I have done her story justice. Margaret Walker wanted to share her life story, her song, with the world. That was my purpose—to assist in the completion of that project. My secondary purpose was for this book to help erase the moniker of "the most famous person nobody knows" and introduce her to a new generation of readers.

Carolyn J. Brown
Jackson, Mississippi

Song of My Life

1. Childhood

Creativity on Display

It seems as if I have always known all my life that I wanted to be a writer.
—Margaret Walker, unpublished autobiography

$\mathcal{W}$hen Margaret Walker was a twelve-year-old girl, she received two gifts from her father which instilled a love of literature and motivated her to write. First, he gave her a small book entitled *Four Lincoln Poets* that included the poems of, most notably, the Harlem Renaissance poet Langston Hughes. It was, she says in her unpublished autobiography, "my first acquaintance with Langston Hughes' poetry," and was a seminal moment in the development of the writer, as young Margaret would have the opportunity to meet the renowned poet four years later. The second gift was a datebook in which her father encouraged her to keep all her poems together. Margaret describes her early poetic attempts as primarily on the subjects of "nature, race, and religion," anticipating the themes she would return to the rest of her life. In her autobiography she recalls her early dedication to poetry and the expense of continuing to purchase journals after she filled that first datebook:

> During my adolescence and teen-age years I wrote some kind of poetry or doggerel every day. And at fourteen and fifteen I was publishing poetry and prose in the local school papers. When I was thirteen I began the habit of keeping journals in composition books which I bought first for a nickel or a dime and gradually they cost a quarter and [then] a dollar.

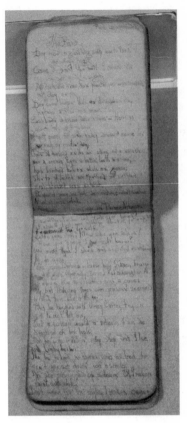

Page from one of Margaret Walker's earliest journals, January 1930, when she was fourteen years old. Walker had copied Paul Laurence Dunbar's poem "The Party."

Margaret's hard work during those four years paid off, as she would meet her poetic hero at New Orleans University (today Dillard University) and show him her poems. In 1932 Langston Hughes was on a lecture tour in the South, and had written Dr. Otto E. Kriege, president of the university, that he would like to read his poetry at one of the black colleges in New Orleans. The two other black schools in the city, Straight and Xavier, had both declined, and Dr. Kriege, according to Walker, "was inclined to join them." She remembers President Kriege saying that he couldn't possibly "conceive of a hundred people coming out to hear a Negro read poetry." She begged her parents to get Hughes to come because, she told them, "I have never seen a real live poet." Her parents, teachers at the university and lovers of literature themselves, agreed, and went to work to guarantee an audience of at least one hundred people and to raise enough money to pay Hughes's one-hundred-dollar fee. Margaret recalls the results of that hard work:

At home and school under Mama's direction, we wrote 800 letters to prominent citizens and schools, clubs, churches, and other organizations in New Orleans. [A]nd that night we packed the auditorium with nearly a thousand people who had paid from fifty and seventy-five cents to a dollar, and he sold at least two hundred dollars worth of books.

Margaret writes in her journal that "I have never forgotten that evening. Every minute detail was forever printed on my brain. The weather began fair but later it rained. I had a new white dress, two piece, of a nubby knit fabric and it was long below my knee. Mercedes [Margaret's younger sister] was playing [piano] on the program and both of us were in the singing directed by Mama."

Journal of Margaret Walker, written while she was a senior at Northwestern, age nineteen, from July to December 1934. Her name and address in New Orleans are printed on the front.

Another journal of Margaret Walker, which covers January–July 1935 and March–July 1936. Her name is written on the bottom.

And singing in the program wasn't even the best part of the evening. Hughes read poems that Mercedes and Margaret had both memorized and that would become "lifetime favorites": "Negro Dancers," "The Weary Blues," "The Negro Mother," and "When Sue Wears Red." Margaret was determined to show Hughes her own poetic efforts as well. She had brought her poems to the reading, carefully concealed, and after she had gone through the receiving line three times but lacked the courage to speak to him, Margaret's mother intervened. Margaret describes the moment:

The first time I went through the line with my sister, Mercedes, I would not lift my eyes and I mumbled a greeting and passed on. Next, my English teacher went through with me to introduce me properly, but I still lost my tongue. Hopeless, I stood aside while people crowded around and he drank about five cups of fruit punch. Finally, when he and my mother were settling up the money, I plunged forward again and Daddy tried lamely but apologetically to tell him I wrote poetry. But it was Mama who remembered why she had gone through all this work, who told him I had my notebook with me and wouldn't he just take a look at some of my things and see if they were any good. He politely consented and then standing by the piano in Peck's Hall Reception Room he did begin to read my poems one after another and he said they were quite good.

Langston Hughes, third from left, in Chapel Hill, North Carolina. This photograph was taken in December 1931 while he was at the University of North Carolina on his lecture tour.

That memorable night Margaret Walker's journey to become a poet officially began.

The sixteen-year-old tongue-tied girl that Langston Hughes met that New Orleans night had her mother and father to thank not only for that momentous introduction and lifetime memory, but also for providing her the opportunity for an education that not all black children were fortunate enough to receive in the South in the 1920s and 1930s. Margaret's early education began in Meridian, Mississippi. Her parents, Sigismund and Marion Walker, were Methodists and making a living teaching at Methodist schools in the South. They had started their married life and teaching careers in Birmingham, Alabama. Sigismund, originally from Jamaica, came to the United States in 1908 in order to become a Methodist minister. After studying first at the Tuskegee Institute alongside Booker T. Washington and George Washington Carver, he transferred to Gammon Theological Seminary in Atlanta where he received his degree in 1913. Margaret explains in a 1982 interview that her father "had no great admiration and respect for either Booker T. Washington or George Washington Carver, or any of the other people at Tuskegee. He felt they were flunkies and toadies to the white man, you see; they were the great compromisers.... [M]y father greatly admired [W. E. B.] Du Bois and everything he stood for [and he was in Atlanta]." His first job following graduation from divinity school was as an interim supply pastor in Pensacola, Florida, which is where he met Margaret's mother, Marion

Portrait of Reverend Sigismund Walker.

Dozier. Margaret herself described their first meeting in this 1982 interview:

On the way [to Pensacola] he met my maternal grandmother on the train, and she told him that her daughter played for the church where he was going. Her daughter was her oldest child, and my aunt. My mother was away in school at the time, in Washington, and when she came home that summer, my father saw her for the first time and fell in love at first sight. They were married the next year; and the night they were married they went to Birmingham, Alabama, where my father pastored the Second Church, as they called it then, in Enon Ridge, where all four of their children were born.

Margaret Walker's mother, Marion (bottom right). This photograph of Marion Dozier Walker is from the faculty page of the New Orleans University 1931 yearbook.

Margaret, the firstborn, was born on July 7, 1915, at 5:00 in the morning, and she writes in her autobiography about the significance of being born on the seventh day of the seventh month of the year: "Both my parents were their mothers' seventh offspring. Both were born in July, the seventh month of the year, and my grandmother says I was born lucky because I was born to them on the seventh day of the seventh month. Our birthdays fall seven days apart. I say seven is my lucky number." Numerology may suggest that the number seven would bring good fortune to Margaret during her lifetime, but the reality for Margaret immediately after she was born was that her father was struggling as a preacher to support

Portrait of Margaret Walker's grandmother, Elvira Ware Dozier.

his growing family. Marion, therefore, just six weeks after Margaret's birth, started teaching music at the Central Alabama Institute, a Methodist school in Mason City, Alabama. Margaret's grandmother,

Central Building, Haven Institute, Meridian, Mississippi.

Elvira Ware Dozier, recently widowed, came to live with her daughter and husband in order to help with baby Margaret.

Five years later, the president of the Haven Institute in Meridian, Mississippi, Dr. R. N. Brooks, a former classmate of Margaret's father at Gammon Theological Seminary in Atlanta, offered both Sigismund and Marion teaching positions at Haven, a Methodist school. The move to Meridian occurred after Margaret had turned five, and the Walkers lived in a dormitory on the school's campus. It was affordable housing as well as a safer residential option for the black family in 1920s Mississippi. Going to school was relatively easy for Margaret since they lived on the campus; after observing children going to school, she simply told her father that she wanted to go, too. He agreed even though in 1920 starting school at age five was very young. However, she was already reading, and she remembers that year in Meridian as a "happy year . . . [as] I stayed that year in the first grade but I read with the fourth grade children."

Even though Meridian was a happy memory for Margaret, it was not for Margaret's mother. Margaret writes that "Mama says now, like her mother before her, she never cared for life in Mississippi," and she believes it is because of something that happened to her, although Margaret never discovered what it was:

Mama says when they first went to Meridian Daddy cautioned her about going anywhere alone. He told her when she wanted to go to town or shopping he would go with her. One day she disregarded this and went alone into the town. I don't know whether it was the way

the white people talked to her, whether she was jostled or what happened, but she never went alone again. In fact she says she remained
on the campus most of the time, from that day forward, and that she
breathed a sigh of relief when they went back to Birmingham.

Even though Marion was relieved to be moving away from
Mississippi, Birmingham would not be as safe and secure as she
remembered.

Margaret continued her education in Birmingham, but it would
not be as simple as in Meridian, where she attended school on the
campus where her family lived. The move back to Birmingham finally allowed the Walkers to purchase their first house, but it was in
a rural area outside of town. Despite the location, owning a home,
after years of living in rented rooms, dormitories, and Methodist par-
sonages, was "a real achievement," Margaret recalls. With three bed-
rooms, a bathroom, electricity, telephone, and hot water, the small
house was the most modern dwelling in which the Walker family
had ever resided. Margaret's favorite room was the front room "with
two large oak chairs, a library table, and two small walls that were
covered with books. It was my favorite hiding place. I would take
a book and hide under a chair and read myself to sleep. Grandma
would call me to come and wash dishes and I wouldn't answer. I

The Walker House, South Fifteenth Place, Southwest (today this is 1320 Fifteenth
Place, Southwest), Birmingham, Alabama. A note in the property file indicates that
it burned in 1952.

never read all the books in that room but I formed a great admiration and awe for books at that time." Margaret also loved the huge yard, and the small orchard her grandmother planted "which soon bore fruit, peaches from May until September, winter pears, black wild cherries, plus a wonderful vegetable garden."

However, since the new home was located in a rural area outside the city, Margaret now had to travel farther to school. When Margaret was seven, she was attending a school in Birmingham that required her to walk "a long way through a white neighborhood on the paved streets to the car line at Dabbs Drugstore and there [she] rode the trolley downtown." One day, Margaret recalls, "three little white boys jumped on me and beat me on my way home. Some colored men were working on the street and they looked on saying nothing. A white man holl[er]ed 'pick up a stick and hit 'em back' but then the colored men spoke and said—'no, don't you do it.'" Margaret didn't fight back because, as she remembers her grandmother telling an acquaintance, "she don't know how to hit back—we don't teach our children to fight."

Despite the challenges, Margaret fondly remembers life in Birmingham during this time. Margaret's brother, Sigismund, Jr., was born, and she recalls that after three girls "Daddy was so happy when Brother was born. He woke us up with Brother in his arms. He couldn't wait till we got up to see the baby. At last they had a boy! . . . [P]eople couldn't call us the three little Walker sisters [anymore] because we were four and one was a boy. That boy was surely going to be spoiled!"

And home provided a safe and secure sanctuary where Margaret's creativity flourished. She recalls how she often played alone because her sister Mercedes only wanted to play piano. She tells Ruth Campbell in a 1983 interview:

> As a very young child, my mother said I would come in from school and . . . even in the wintertime, I would put on a hat and go out in the backyard in my coat and hat and talk to all my imaginary playmates. My sister didn't want to play [outside]. She wanted to play the piano all the time. And so I, yes, I invented playmates. Miss Choomby is one of [my] invented playmates. [I] played Miss Anne and Miss Choomby. Miss Ann[e] was the white lady, and Miss Choomby was the black lady, and [I] took turns being Miss Ann[e] and Miss Choomby.

In another instance, on Margaret's ninth birthday she put together an operetta, "The Golden Whistle," and all the neighborhood children had parts in it. In her autobiography, Margaret explains how she directed the production:

> Mama was always getting samples of musical materials for teaching from Presser and Company in Philadelphia and this was one that Mercedes and I liked so we decided to put it on. Mercedes could play the music and I could direct it and see that everybody learned his part, his dance, and his songs. A boy named Steve sang the leading solo:
>
> *Alas, alas, ah woe is me*
> *What evil has my pathway crossed?*
> *This summer day grows dark and drear.*
> *My golden whistle has been lost.*
>
> A white rabbit stole the whistle.
> My youngest sister was a butterfly and [we gathered] branches from the woods to be [used] for scenery and Japanese lanterns strung across the lawn and even the piano moved out on the porch. It was my birthday party so there had to be ice cream and cake but the play was my present. Even the church folks next door left their fish-fry and came to be our audience. And it was a huge success. And [M]ama said nobody but Margaret could cook up something like that. And as she said, "You had started it and there was nothing for us to do but go along with it." Oddly enough, that is the wonderful thing my parents have always done. They went along with the program.

Margaret and her siblings enjoyed this house and yard for only four years. Sadly, the Central Alabama Institute where both her parents were teaching burned down. With both her parents employed at the Methodist school, Margaret writes:

> That fire was to change our lives completely. Neither Daddy nor Mama had a job and we had only been in our home a little while. Daddy got a job teaching at Industrial High School in Birmingham

Brainerd Hall, Central Alabama Institute, Birmingham, Alabama.

and at night he worked in a [t]ailor shop in Ensley and on Sundays he preached. He seemed to be gone all the time but at night as soon as he put his foot on the porch Mama knew his footstep and would cry out in relief, "Rev Walker?" and Daddy tired but happy to be home would answer "yes."

Struggling to make ends meet, Sigismund accepted a job teaching at New Orleans University. He would be there a year before the rest of his family would join him. Margaret says in her autobiography that the move to New Orleans at the age of ten marked "[t]he end of my childhood. . . . I was sad about leaving Birmingham and all my friends I had learned to love so well. I felt I would never see most of them again."

2. Education

New Orleans and Chicago

I am sure going to Northwestern was the making of me.
—*Margaret Walker, unpublished autobiography*

$\mathcal{N}$ew Orleans was a city unlike any ten-year-old Margaret had ever seen before. When the family arrived by train, Margaret was immediately struck by the Crescent City's size and urban feel. In Birmingham, the Walker family had lived on the outskirts of town; in New Orleans they lived right in its heart, near New Orleans University, where her father was teaching and where her mother would soon join the faculty as a music instructor. Although Margaret missed her big backyard with all the fruit trees, she and Mercedes liked being able to walk to their new school, Gilbert Academy.

New Orleans is where Margaret Walker's education seriously began. At the age of ten, she was placed in the seventh grade. She quickly moved up to the ninth grade and Margaret recalls the "great excitement of studying the French Revolution. For the first time I learned about Robespierre, Danton, Marat and Marie Antoinette. I was completely taken by the slogans 'liberté, égalité, fraternité.'" In fall 1927, only twelve years old, Margaret entered the tenth grade and while she was studying "Latin—Caesar—English Literature, History and Geometry . . . I spent all the time I could reading and writing."

Margaret's poetic and oratorical talents were beginning to bring her attention. During her twelfth-grade year, she was awarded a leather-bound Bible for an oration she gave on "the American Negro's Obligation to Africa." What was special about the Bible was not only

College Song

Marion D. Walker

Down in dear old Louisiana
Waves a blue and golden banner
'Tis the emblem of dear N. O. U.
The best, the finest school for you.
There the sun is always shining
There you'll never find repining
It's a great and noble college
We are proud to sing its name.

CHORUS

New Orleans   I love New Orleans
I love her halls and her campus green
Boys there are strong and steady steady
Girls there are finest seen—rah rah! rah rah
Sun there is always shining. shining.
Skies there are always blue, rah! rah rah!
New Orleans. I love New Orleans, and
I'm always going to love her too, rah! rah!

You may brag of being stucky
You may boast of being plucky
But, O boy indeed you are lucky
If you go to dear N. O. U
With her beauty pointing upward
Stalwart. strong. her cry is onward
Marching on and on to victory
Building, lifting as we climb.

CHORUS

COLLEGE YELL

Leader   'Hey boy
Rabble   'Hey
C. L.   'Hey Boy
R   'Hey
C. R.   ''What's the matter with the team?'
R   'It's alright.
C. L.   'Who said so?
R   'Everybody
C. L.   'Who is everybody?'
R   'N O. U
To-gether   Team—team—bully for the team, rah-rah-rah.
             Team—team--bully for the team rah-tah-rah.

HAND AND FOOT CLAP

Tick-A-tick-tic-tic-tic
Tic-et-a-tick-tic-tic
  Tic-A-tick. tick-A-tic
    Bam!

Marion Walker wrote the New Orleans University college song.

Sigismund Walker, front center, with the Melden
Dramatic Club, New Orleans University.

Marion Walker, front right, with the university orchestra, New Orleans University.

Sigismund Walker, bottom left, faculty
page, New Orleans University.

her name and the date engraved in gold on the cover, but that it came
from her father's alma mater, Gammon Theological Seminary, which
presented the prize annually. When she was awarded the Bible from
Dean Hayes, Margaret remembers him telling her that "'If you will
let this Bible guide your life, you will not only find what a wonderful
book it is, you will have a wonderful life.' I believed him and until I
was twenty-one years old I never missed a day reading that Bible."

Margaret and her sister Mercedes were not the only ones going to
school during this time. Both Sigismund and Marion were encouraged to get their higher education degrees since they were teaching
at the college level. They decided to attend Northwestern University
in Chicago because it was a Methodist school and they could go at a
reduced price. Even though her father still did not think he could af-
ford it and Margaret recalls that he even cried at the thought of leaving his family in New Orleans, Marion packed his steamer trunk and
pushed her husband out the door. Finally, Sigismund, after studying
for six weeks every summer between 1924 and 1929 (the only summer he missed was 1927 when Marion needed an operation), graduated from Northwestern with a master's degree in biblical literature.
Marion, too, earned a college degree from Northwestern, but not her
master's; Margaret recalls that "she said we were at the wrong age for

her to leave us at home, even with grandma who kept us the [one] summer Mama went to [finish] school. So, my mother gave up her chance to get an advanced degree."

Even though both her parents attended Northwestern, it was not the obvious choice for Margaret after she graduated from Gilbert Academy at age fourteen. She continued her education at New Orleans University, where both her parents were on the faculty. She added to her impressive list of academic accomplishments by winning the freshman composition prize (a five-dollar gold piece), which she recalls as being hard earned:

My teacher, Miss Ella Fluke, was a white woman who had graduated from Northwestern. I thought she was a very hard teacher because she did not give me all A grades on my compositions and I was accustomed to mak[ing] A[s]. She gave me B grades and would point out that I was too flowery and did not use the exact word to get the precise shade of meaning. I loved words like "phantasmagoria" and I would never use a simple monosyllabic word if I could find a polysyllabic word instead.

GILBERT ACADEMY (High School).
12th Grade

Allen, Bernice C.	New Orleans
Alston, Helen G.	New Orleans
Barnes, Bonnie B.	Alexandria, La.
Berkley, Carrie B.	New Orleans
Berry, Frank, Jr.	Alexandria, La.
Booker, Wilbert	Leesville, La.
Brown, Barney B.	New Orleans
Brown, Luella	Angie, La.
Coleman, Mary Louise	Baldwin, La.
Cooper, Orestra	Amory, Miss.
Danks, Wilbert J.	Houma, La.
Dials, Elva Nita	Lake Charles, La.
Dennison, Grant A.	Kenner, La.
Edinburgh, Benjamin S.	New Orleans
Ellis, Ernestine	Moss Point, Miss.
Francois, Adam	New Orleans
Gardner, Pearl S.	New Orleans
Gray, Henry W.	New Orleans
Green, Harold B.	New Orleans
Green, Jerome G.	New Orleans
Green, Mary Thelma	New Orleans
Hartman, Alvin J.	Lake Charles, La.
Henderson, Roy James	Lecompte, La.
Hoskins, Herbert W.	Morgan City, La.
Houston, Beulah Mae	New Orleans
Hunter, James Lincoln	New Orleans
Jacobs, Leon, Jr.	New Orleans
Moore, John	New Orleans
Morgan, Jerome	Meridian, Miss.
Points, Lucy Eloise	Marion, Ala.
Polk, Alberta	Prentiss, Miss.
Porter, Augustine	New Orleans
Raphael, Henry	New Orleans
Reddix, Joseph W. Jr.	Shreveport, La.
Reed, Elzie	Bassfield, Miss.
Reid, Virtia Mae	Biloxi, Miss.
Robinson, Gertrude A.	New Orleans
Robinson, Neely	New Orleans
Savage, Myrtle M.	New Orleans
Scott, Annie Belle	New Orleans
Smith, Alcheous	McGhee, Ark.
Thomas, Frances No. 1	Lacompte, La.
Thompson, Joseph Thickield	Denham Springs, La.
Tuckerson, Carrie Mae	Amite, La.
Turner, Hilda Etta	New Orleans
Walker, Margaret A.	New Orleans
Walmsley, Rosa B.	Morgan City, La.
Washington, Ruby	Beaumont, Texas
Wiley, Helen B.	New Orleans
Williams, Lillie B.	New Orleans

Sigismund Walker wearing his graduation robes from Northwestern University.

Margaret Walker's name on the twelfth-grade list, Gilbert Academy.

Main Building, New Orleans University.

Sigismund and Marion considered sending Margaret away to college at age fifteen, and even paid the five-dollar room deposit to Talladega College, the oldest private historically black college in Alabama. However, Margaret recalls that two people stopped them from proceeding further with their plans: their pastor, Reverend J. W. E. Bowen, Jr., and the white president of New Orleans University, Dr. Otto E. Kriege. Rev. Bowen cautioned Margaret's parents about sending her away to college so young: "Are you thinking about letting Margaret go away from home as young as she is? You have a nice young girl and when she comes back she'll be smoking and drinking and everything else." And, according to Margaret, that thought "shook Daddy up." Dr. Kriege's argument was based less on Margaret's age and more on the type of school she should attend: he said "that if they were thinking about sending me away to college it did not make sense to send me to another black college in the South, unless they thought New Orleans University wasn't as good as any other college. If I were to go away, they should send me to a white school." Northwestern then became Margaret's college destination, especially after Sigismund and Marion went during the summers in the late 1920s and earned their degrees there.

Fortunately, Margaret did not have to go to college alone. Her sister Mercedes went as well, as Marion felt that she had already taught her piano prodigy "all the music she could." And when Sigismund had second thoughts about sending the girls to the northern school because of the expense, Marion insisted, because

President Otto E. Kriege, New Orleans University.

Margaret, she reminded him, was "losing interest in school altogether because [she] was no longer challenged enough to study and all [she] wanted to do was write poetry, filling [her] dime and quarter composition books with drivel." That convinced him, and in mid-August 1932 the Walker family—Daddy, Mama, Margaret, Mercedes, and Sigismund, Jr.—set out for Evanston, Illinois.

The 950-mile car trip from New Orleans to Evanston was not easy in 1932. The roads in Louisiana and Mississippi "were all dust and gravel with almost no concrete." Margaret recalls in her autobiography that "[w]e carried food, water, and a five gallon can of gasoline

Margaret Walker's application for admission to Northwestern University.

Sundown Town sign, c. 1875–1899.

in the car with us, because we dared not stop at a strange white filling station." Blacks traveling through Mississippi had to be especially careful:

> Of course there were no rest rooms along the road to accommodate us. . . . We rode until we found a black filling station and my father sought out a fellow Methodist minister hoping we could stop and rest a while at the parsonage. But the minister's wife was not friendly. She sat on the front porch and did not ask us inside. . . . Our next stop was Memphis, Tennessee [where] my parents sought out Church friends where we spent the night after a good hot supper and hot baths. We made it to Paris, Illinois by midnight so we parked on the side of the road and slept in the car. Southern Illinois had a legendary sign that said: "Nigger, don't let the sun go down with you in this town."

The roads improved the farther north they traveled, but Margaret recalls that in August the sun was "broiling hot and on the paved roads we would feel the intense heat worse than on the dust and gravel which threatened to choke us." It wasn't until the Walkers arrived in Chicago that they could relax and breathe easy again.

In Evanston, Margaret's parents had arranged for the girls to live as boarders with Lyda Landers at 812 Emerson St., where they could walk "straight up the street into Emerson gate and into University Hall." The girls were ages seventeen (Margaret) and fifteen (Mercedes), and Sigismund left Mrs. Landers with the following instructions: "They don't dance or play cards; they don't receive company; and see that they are in bed every night by ten o'clock." And then he took his leave, with his teenage daughters in their pajamas looking through the screen door, and drove back home with the others to New Orleans. Margaret says of that moment: "[F]or the first time in my life I felt desolate and a long way from home."

Main card catalog, Deering Library, Northwestern University.

Reading Room, Deering Library, Northwestern University.

Exterior, Deering Library, Northwestern University.

The subject of Margaret's first poem in Chicago was her new hometown. Written on September 3, 1932, and simply entitled "Chicago," she describes her first impressions of this big, intimidating city:

I shall remember Chicago
from the first, as being:
A place of settling dust and grime;
Of alleys running through the town
Of motorists who drive at mad-cap speed
Of yiddish women wearing black head shawls
Of brightly lighted streets
And great sky-sweeping shops
And of long ugly winding steps
At the backways of tenement houses.

Margaret was not only intimidated by the city of Chicago, but by Northwestern as well. She writes that "[t]hose first few weeks at Northwestern Mercedes and I were awed by the greatness of the University. Deering Library was new and I would stare up at the ceilings which seemed full of oak leaves and acorns hand carved of wood. We went to convocations and found our way around in downtown Evanston with great trepidation."

Several reasons may account for Margaret's fear of and discomfort at the university: first, Margaret and Mercedes had only been away from home once before—to summer camp in Waveland, Mississippi; second, Margaret recalls there were only "forty Negroes that year in an enrollment of 11,000 students in the University"; third, racism was rampant and "teachers told darky jokes openly in the classroom and when white students laugh you burned with shame but you could do nothing about it"; fourth, the young girls had no money and "were at the mercy of everybody." Margaret remembers depending on a neighbor, Mrs. Godwin, for meals, as well as a friend of her parents she affectionately called Aunt Hattie. In addition, the girls looked forward to a weekly care package from their grandmother in New Orleans that had "meat, chicken, pies and cake."

One other element of anxiety was the curriculum itself. Margaret quickly realized she was not as prepared for college as she thought she was. Even though she entered Northwestern as a junior, she had to "take several sophomore English courses that first year" as well as zoology ("which I was very grateful to pass") and two years of Greek that, she writes, "nearly killed me." She enjoyed the literature classes, though, taking modern poetry, British and American literature, and world literature, where she read for the first time "Aristotle's *Poetics*, Plato's *Republic*, . . . Aeschylus, Sophocles and Euripides; Dante's *Divine Comedy*, Goethe's *Faust*, . . . and Strindberg's plays; Boccaccio's *Decameron*, Rabelais' *Gargantua and Pantagruel*, and Voltaire's *Candide*." She writes in her autobiography that she "devoured them" and "[t]his began a long and continued friendship with these writers of the Western World."

She also found her first true mentor at Northwestern, Professor E. B. Hungerford. According to Walker's biographer Maryemma Graham, Hungerford shaped and directed Margaret's education:

> Under Hungerford, she learned all the forms of English poetry and the English metrical system; she learned how to do the scansion of a poem and memorized the versification patterns. She read the English poets, focusing on the Romantic writers, and developed a keen interest in Shakespearean sonnets, the odes of Shelley and Keats, and the long poems of Wordsworth, all important influences upon her future work.

During Margaret's senior year at Northwestern, Hungerford taught her creative writing as well, and under his tutelage, she wrote a long poem on the pirate Jean Lafitte, several short stories, and three hundred pages of *Jubilee*, her Civil War novel. Graham describes the scene when Margaret went to Professor Hungerford's office for her final grade:

> When she turned in her poems to him along with her first three hundred pages of *Jubilee*, she went to his office to find out her grade. Thinking that she had failed miserably, she asked what she would have to do to get an "A." Hungerford not only awarded her the highest grade in the course but provided her with a host of little magazines and poetry reviews, suggesting some places where she submit some of her work. One of the magazines was *Poetry*; its editor, Harriet Monroe, had been one of the speakers she heard at Northwestern. She secretly vowed that she would publish there.

Perhaps the greatest gift Professor Hungerford gave to Margaret, though, was managing to get his African American student inducted into the all-white Northwestern chapter of the Poetry Society of America. Not only did her inclusion in the chapter give the young writer literary credibility and respect, but Graham mentions in a footnote to her essay "I Want to Write, I Want to Write the Songs of My People: The Emergence of Margaret Walker," that "[a]pparently Hungerford had broken a racial barrier by lobbying for Walker to be the first African American to be admitted in a college chapter."

Before graduating from Northwestern, Margaret had the opportunity to hear W. E. B. Du Bois speak. Unlike her encounter with Langston Hughes four years earlier, this time Margaret found the courage to talk to her father's hero about her poetry: "I went up to speak to [Du Bois] after his speech. He was a cordial but quite reserved person. I remember how his quiet dignity impressed me.

William Edward Burghardt Du Bois, c. 1910–1930.

Even then he was bald and wore a little Van Dyke beard, a very small man, reminding me physically of my own father, but striking and imposing in his presence."

Like Hughes, Du Bois encouraged the young writer and invited Margaret to submit a poem to his magazine, *The Crisis*. She did, and "Daydream" was accepted and published in 1934:

> *I want to write.*
> *I want to write the songs of [my] people.*
> *I want to hear them singing melodies in the dark.*
> *I want to catch the last floating strains*
> *From their sob-stricken throats.*
> *I want to frame their dreams into words,*
> *Their souls into notes.*
> *I want to catch their sunshine laughter in a bowl;*
> *Fling dark hands to a darker sky*
> *And fill them full of stars,*
> *Then crush and mix such lights till they become*
> *A mirrored pool of brilliance in the dawn.*

Already a published poet, Margaret would graduate from Northwestern a few months later, unsure of her next steps but more committed to her writing than ever before.

3. Chicago

Richard Wright and the South Side Writers' Group

Chicago was a testing time of pain and hardship and fiery trial. I was no
longer starry-eyed and eager and I am sure I had lost some of my idealism if
not optimism. But it was also a glorious time to be alive and to come of age.
—Margaret Walker, unpublished autobiography

*W*hen Margaret Walker graduated from Northwestern in 1935,
the world was in political turmoil. Margaret writes in her autobiography that "Italy was moving into Ethiopia ... Civil War broke out in
Spain and I remember the thirties ... as a time when there were rallies
held everywhere." In Chicago, Margaret met young people, in their
twenties like herself, moved to action and leaving the States to volun-
teer on the dangerous frontlines of these war zones. Margaret did not
go, but following graduation was determined to stay in Chicago and
work. For seven months, Margaret and Mercedes looked for jobs, but
it was the Depression and times were hard. Margaret recalls one job
they found that only lasted a single day:

> We went to work picking nuts in a pecan factory but after a day we
> were fired. The floorlady said we were no good and she couldn't be
> bothered. I was relieved. I thought Mercedes would ruin her hands
> and not be able to play the piano. She was also relieved. She was
> afraid I would cut my hands and be unable to type and write! I
> walked twelve miles one day looking for work and all I got that day
> was a pair of fallen arches. My feet have never been the same since.

Richard Wright, 1940.

After they were fired, the only money the girls made came from "a few dollars [Mercedes earned] as organist for the neighborhood Methodist Church where we worshipped . . . [and] a little money [Margaret] made typing." It wasn't until the girls met Dr. Jay I. Peters through the pastor of their church that their luck changed.

Dr. Peters was a friend of Margaret's parents and had known the girls in New Orleans. They did not remember him, but he remembered them, and Margaret recalls his words when he found them in Chicago: "You don't remember me but the last time I saw you you were children in New Orleans. I know you. 'I'm going to get you a job,' he said to me, and to Mercedes, 'You are going back to school.'" And he delivered on his promises, helping Margaret get a job with the Works Progress Administration's Federal Writers' Project and enrolling Mercedes at the city's Central YMCA College for the second semester in order for her to attend music school and finish college.

The Works Progress Administration (WPA), where Margaret went to work, was created by President Franklin D. Roosevelt to generate jobs for people during the Great Depression. It offered opportunities to millions to carry out public works projects, including the construction of public buildings and roads, as well as arts, drama, media, and literacy projects. For Margaret, this job not only provided financial relief; it introduced her to a world of writers in Chicago she never knew existed before.

Margaret's new position with the WPA was located in an office on Erie Street near Lake Michigan, but even better than the view of the lake was its proximity to the office of a magazine Margaret was familiar with from Northwestern: "[W]e were on the same street as the Office of *Poetry* magazine. . . . I knew about *Poetry* and its Editor-Founder from my college days. I heard Harriet Monroe read her poetry one night . . . and I hoped someday to publish in *Poetry*." According to Maryemma Graham, the WPA job provided Margaret with unique opportunities; she met the current editor of *Poetry*, George Dillon, as well as "radical white women poets like Leonie Adams, Elinor Wylie, Louise Bogan, and Muriel Rukeyser."

Perhaps the most important relationship that developed during this period was her friendship with novelist Richard Wright. Margaret had heard about a writers' group through the National Negro Congress (NNC), "in which the Communist party assumed an aggressive role of leadership." Graham explains how Communist ideals took hold in 1930s Chicago, especially among blacks and writers, like Wright:

> In Chicago, home to one of the largest urban populations and distinctively black and southern in character, the Depression fueled the activities of the Communist Party, which drew a host of writers into its orbit. . . . The Communist Party especially targeted artists and writers, encouraging representation of the masses of people, whether, black, ethnic, or poor. It was the writers who would impart their vision of a new America to the nation and the world.

Wright was involved with the National Negro Congress, a group that attempted to build a national constituency to pressure New

Deal administrators for labor and civil rights. According to the *Encyclopedia of Chicago*,

> Over 800 delegates, 43 percent of them from Chicago and the rest
> from across the nation, representing 500 different organizations,
> filled the Eighth Regiment Armory on the Chicago's South Side for
> the inauguration of the NNC from February 14 to 16, 1936. A large
> crowd gathered outside the armory to listen to the proceedings on
> loudspeakers, and WCFL, "The [Radio] Voice of Labor," broadcast
> highlights of the event over the airwaves. The sessions included dis-
> cussions concerning sharecroppers, interracial organizing, women
> and labor, the arts, business, and the war in Ethiopia. The *Chicago
> Defender* accurately assessed the event as "the most ambitious effort
> for bringing together members of the Race on any single issue."

Margaret heard about the rally from an advertisement in the news-
paper, and attended a planning session with members of her church.
Her desire to attend the meeting had nothing to do with the congress, however; she had heard that Langston Hughes would be there
and she desired to see him again. And again she brought poems for
him to look at, but this time he refused:

> I tried to press my manuscripts on Langston, but . . . he would not
> take them. Instead he turned to [Richard] Wright, who was standing
> nearby, listening to the conversation and smiling at my desperation.
> Langston said, "If you people get a [writing] group together, don't for-
> get to include this girl." Wright promised that he would remember.

And two months later he did. Margaret recalls receiving a penny
postcard in the mail inviting her to the first official meeting of the
South Side Writers' Group.

In her biography of Wright, entitled *Richard Wright, Daemonic
Genius*, Margaret describes her anxiety over this meeting and her
first impressions of Wright:

> Twice I left the house and turned back, the first time out of great
> self-consciousness because I felt I looked abominable. I had nothing
> to wear to make a nice appearance, and I was going to the far South

Side, where I felt people would make fun of me. But my great desire to meet writers and end my long isolation conquered this superficial fear. I made myself go. When I arrived at the address given on the card, I discovered I was very late. . . . I heard a man expounding on the sad state of Negro writing at that point in the thirties, and he was punctuating his remarks with pungent epithets. I drew back in Sunday-school horror, totally shocked by his strong speech, but I steeled myself to hear him out. The man was Richard Wright. Later, each person present was asked to bring something to read next time, but most people refused. When I was asked, I said, rather defiantly, that I would. I left the meeting alone.

Margaret had never met anyone before like Richard Wright. She was amazed by his education, which came from his own reading, and not from attending high school or college:

I asked [Wright] what his academic background was and he delighted in answering me with relish, "What you mean? Where I went to school? I didn't go to school. I haven't been any further than the ninth grade. I went over to Englewood once and started to go back to high school but I soon found out I didn't belong there. I was bored stiff." Well, I was flabbergasted. I couldn't believe him. And when I read stories, fiction he was writing, I was even more flabbergasted. He must be joking, he couldn't be telling the truth. This man was completely educated, more literate than many of my fellow classmates and college graduates. Where did he get such an education? I soon found out though he never told me. He was a Marxist and he had gotten a Marxist education in Chicago. His serious reading of literature and books began in Memphis . . . but his Marxist education in history, economics, and political science, psychology, and philosophy came from the Marxists, the young Jewish intellectuals, or the young lions he knew in Chicago and all of it in the thirties.

Margaret shared a few of her poems at the next meeting of the South Side Writers' Group, and "was surprised to see they did not cut me down." Two members, she recalled, "were kind in their praise," and Wright even walked part of the way home with Margaret after the meeting. He told her he was going to join her on the WPA

Writers' Project, and the following week when Margaret reported for work he was there: "... Wright was the first person I saw when I got off the elevator. He quickly came over and led me to his desk. He was a supervisor, and I was a junior writer. My salary was $85 per month, while his was $125.... A year later I advanced to $94."

As a junior writer, Margaret was responsible for articles in the *Illinois Guide Book*, news stories, and coverage of art exhibits. She did not have to work in the office, but when she did check in, she remembers, "I spent most of the day in conversation with Wright." Conversation with Wright, Margaret describes in her autobiography, was an education in itself:

> ... I recognized at once that he was an intellectual giant and I always found his conversation fascinating. And we talked about everything under the sun. We talked about history, people, places, ideas, writing, sex, religion, God, family, marriage, politics, money, race... you name it. We talked for weeks and months, every time we got together, for hours at [a] time. There just wasn't anything we couldn't talk and laugh about. But our friends never could understand that the relationship was purely literary, platonic.

Cover of *Illinois Guide Book*, 1939. Walker worked on the *Illinois Guide Book* while employed as a junior writer for the WPA.

The relationship could be described as similar to a student and teacher, as Wright started giving and recommending books for Margaret to read. Some were Marxist and philosophical—Karl Marx's *Das Kapital*; John Strachey's *The Coming Struggle for Power*; *The Complete Philosophy of Nietzsche*; and Adam Smith's *The Wealth of Nations*—but the majority were literary. Some works Margaret had read before, but Wright was opening her eyes to things she had never noticed on first readings:

One afternoon as we talked Wright quoted from T. S. Eliot:

> *Let us go, then, you and I,*
> *When the evening is spread out against the sky*
> *Like a patient etherized upon a table;*

And he exclaimed, "What an image!" Something exploded in my head, and I went home to find my copy of Louis Untermeyer's anthology, *Modern American Poetry,* and re-read Eliot. I remember how dull he had seemed at Northwestern when the teacher was reading aloud. . . .

I began James Joyce with *Portrait of an Artist as a Young Man* then read *Ulysses.* Wright used Joyce as an example of writing *Lawd Today,* being struck by a book that kept all the action limited to one day. . . .

Stephen Crane's *Red Badge of Courage* I knew, but not *Maggie, Girl of the Streets,* which was Wright's favorite. . . . Reading Proust is an experience I associate completely with Wright. [And reading D. H. Lawrence's] works . . . led to some discussions we had then of Freud, Jung, and Adler, especially of Freud.

Wright not only opened Margaret's mind to books and authors; he encouraged her writing as well, especially her poetry.

Margaret credits Wright with helping her with her free verse form, especially a poetic characteristic that she has become known for:

> We sat together and worked on the forms of my poetry, the free verse things, and came up with my long line or strophic form, punctuated by a short line. I remembered particularly the poem "People of Unrest," which Wright and I revised together, emphasizing the verbs:

> *Stare from your pillow into the sun*
> *See the disk of light in the shadows.*
> *Watch day growing tall*
> *Cry with a loud voice after the sun.*
> *Take his yellow arms and wrap them round your life.*
> *Be glad to be washed in the sun.*
> *Be glad to see.*
> *People of Unrest and sorrow*
> *Stare from your pillow into the sun.*

She also remembers their shared interest in "Negro spirituals and work songs," literary forms which would inform future works of both writers.

Margaret gained confidence in her poetic abilities in the mid 1930s—through her friendship with Wright and inclusion in the South Side Writers' Group—to the point that she submitted her first poems for publication in national magazines since "Daydream" in 1934. She finally achieved her goal of publishing in *Poetry* magazine when "For My People" was selected for the November 1937 issue, followed by "We Have Been Believers" (1938) and "The Struggle Staggers Us" (1939). She also published poems in *Opportunity* and *The New Challenge*. Maryemma Graham believes "Southern Song," published in *The New Challenge*, is reminiscent of the earlier "Daydream" and "moves closer to the form that, in its full evolution, marked [Walker's] signature: the long incremental free-verse stanza in which indented lines explore the meaning of the opening line for each stanza":

> *I want my body bathed again by southern suns; my soul*
> *reclaimed again from southern soil: I want to rest again in*
> *southern fields; in grass and hay and clover bloom; to lay*
> *my hand again upon the clay baked by a southern sun;*
> *to touch the rain-soaked earth and smell the smell of soil.*
> *I want my rest unbroken in the fields of southern earth; freedom*
> *to watch the corn wave silver in the sun and mark the*
> *splashing of a brook—a pond with ducks and frogs;*
> *and count the clouds.*
> *I want no mobs to wrench me from my southern rest; no forms*
> *to take me in the night and burn my shack and make for*
> *me a nightmare full of oil and flame.*
> *I want my careless song to strike no minor key; no fiend to stand*
> *between my body's southern song—the fusion of the*
> *South, my body's [southern] song and me.*

In 1936 the South Side Writers' Group disbanded. Richard Wright, friend and mentor, left Chicago after ten years for New York City, but Margaret remained in Chicago with her sister Mercedes, continuing to work for the WPA and struggling to earn enough money to live and write.

4. Chicago

Life after Northwestern

Thus ended my Chicago years. I had just turned twenty-four and
seven years had passed in Chicago—four years since Northwestern.
Now I was ready to begin a new cycle of my life.
—*Margaret Walker, unpublished autobiography*

*M*argaret Walker's job with the Works Progress Administration
was the primary source of income for the two sisters from 1936 to 1938:

> I was considered the breadwinner on WPA although Mercedes
> certainly had jobs, but I made the money for our food and lodging
> and sometimes enough to pay on Mercedes' tuition and sometimes
> enough to send home to help mama and daddy with utilities and
> house payments and once enough to bring my very young brother to
> Chicago to see Joe Louis fight and go to the Regal [T]heatre to hear
> Chick Webb and Ella Fitzgerald.

Despite their financial hardships, Margaret experienced a wonderful social life during this time, even though Richard Wright had
moved to New York and the South Side Writers' Group no longer
met. One particularly memorable weekend Margaret attended a
cocktail party on a Saturday afternoon at the office of *Poetry* magazine in honor of Muriel Rukeyser, followed by "reading poetry and
talking till the wee hours of the morning." On Sunday, she visited
with a friend, Margaret Goss, who introduced her to the music of
Billie Holiday. Margaret recalls her friend saying, "Listen, Margaret

Billie Holiday. Photographer William P. Gottlieb, February 1947.

Walker, I want you to hear this," and playing "Strange Fruit" on the record player:

Southern trees bear a strange fruit
Blood on the leaves and blood on the root
Black bodies swinging in the Southern breeze
Strange fruit hanging from the poplar trees

Margaret said, "It was the first time I heard that song and it made a deep impression on me. I do not think I have heard a voice exactly like Billie Holiday's and the words of that song follow one through the rest of life." Margaret stayed overnight with her friends the Moultries this same night, and went to work the following Monday morning with Ava Moultrie, who also worked for the WPA. When Margaret returned home Monday afternoon, after being out all night, she vividly remembers Mercedes and her landlady's shocked reactions: "Mercedes was shocked into stony silence and my Landlady also said nothing, but I had a ball and for once I felt entirely free to do as I pleased. Especially since I knew I had really done nothing wrong or reprehensible."

From 1936 to 1939 Margaret enjoyed all that Chicago had to offer. She met poet Gwendolyn Brooks, and Langston Hughes visited frequently. She writes that "rarely did he show up without coming out to our house or inviting me out to lunch at the Grand Hotel and sundry chop and steak houses." She wrote letters to her family back in Louisiana describing in detail her life in Chicago during this time, and returned home after five years in Chicago to see her parents, grandmother, and younger sister and brother. The trip home, like the trip to Northwestern years before, was difficult. Not much had changed for blacks traveling North to South:

We couldn't manage the train fare for both of us so we went on the bus. The trip was fine to Memphis and we slept all night, but in Memphis we changed buses and were put on the back seat behind the leather jim-crow curtain. It was hot summer time and no air was stirring. Down the dusty road we went to Brookhaven, Mississippi, where two young people, brother and sister, invited us to their house across the road where we could have a cold drink of water and stretch our legs. There was no restroom even in the station for us. By the time

A bus showing the separation of whites and blacks.

we got to Hammond, Louisiana I was so sick I was fainting away. The man stopped the bus so that Mercedes could buy me a coca cola, but when we got to New Orleans I was ill enough to be put to bed. Mama and Daddy began at once to plan ways to raise train fare back. There was just no way I could stand the bus trip back to Chicago. So they raised the money. Mercedes and I gave a recital and appeared on radio in Alexandria [Louisiana]; I read poetry and she played and we made our fare back to Chicago.

Upon Margaret's return, there was a letter waiting for her from Richard Wright. Wright was enjoying critical acclaim for his writing; his short story collection, *Uncle Tom's Children* (1938), won first prize in the *Story* magazine contest open to Federal Writers' Project authors for best book-length manuscript. In the letter he asked Margaret to help him gather information on the Robert Nixon case, which he was using to help him write his novel *Native Son*. Wright had become deeply interested in the case of this eighteen-year-old black man accused of murdering a white woman. In a 1982 interview with Claudia Tate, Walker describes assisting Wright with his research:

> I remember Wright wrote me a Special Delivery letter, requesting that I send him all the newspaper clippings on Robert Nixon's trial. I sent him enough to cover a nine by twelve foot floor. Then he came to Chicago and asked me to help him for a day or so. We went to the library, and on my card I got that [Clarence] Darrow book, and I took him to the office of [Ulysses] Keys, who had been the lawyer on the case. I asked Keys for the brief. Those were integral parts of *Native Son*. I still didn't know what his story was about.

Wright was traveling back and forth between New York and Chicago as he worked on the book, and in May 1939 he visited Margaret and encouraged her to come next month to New York City to try and sell her first novel, "Goose Island," about "social conditions in Chicago," and experience a once-in-a-lifetime event: the World's Fair. He even promised to help her find a place to stay. For Margaret it was the final year working for the WPA, and money was, as usual, extremely tight, but her desire to try and sell her first novel at the League of

American Writers meeting and attend the World's Fair prevailed over her anxiety about money—she bought a round-trip railroad ticket and went. Margaret describes seeing Wright when she disembarked from the train:

> It was Saturday morning, June 7, 1939. When I got off the train there was a push of people, but as we walked through the gates I saw Wright looking worriedly for me. His face lighted up with a broad grin and I was slightly relieved. I told him I almost didn't come, and he asked why. I confessed at last I had had money problems and really had no money. He said "Don't worry. I can let you have some. I have a little money." He found

World's Fair, New York City, 1939.

> a cab and said we would go directly to the New School for Social Research where the meetings were going on. . . . I really wanted to go up to Harlem and get out of the clothes I had worn all night on the train, but he said no, so we went, baggage and all to the Village and the New School.
>
> I was not prepared for a bunch of people to walk up to us on the sidewalk as we alighted from the cab and two young white girls said, "Dick, is this your wife? Introduce us to her." He just smiled and said nothing and I said, "Tell them I'm not your wife," but he said "Hush."

In her autobiography, Margaret describes her first trip to New York as a complete disaster. "Young, naive, green, and oh so vulnerable"—Margaret recalls Wright trying to teach her how to roll spaghetti on a spoon—"but I was so awkward I could have cried." She met writer Ralph Ellison and his wife, . . . and had a wonderful time, but was not prepared for the "sophisticated lad[ies]" she was introduced to by Wright and who spurned her acquaintance. Wright also neglected her for days, and it was Langston Hughes who served as a tour guide and "showed me the sights of the City."

After getting lost on the way to the World's Fair because she had to go alone and catching the wrong train back to Chicago, Margaret finally returned home. She writes that "[i]t was a painful experience—one that would hurt for the rest of my life. . . . I had been to see the bright lights and like the candle moths I came too close to the flame and was burned." Her relationship with Wright deteriorated following this trip, and a law had passed ending WPA employment after eighteen months or longer. Margaret had served three years; she had to find something new.

Education seemed to be the answer, and she writes in her autobiography that "I knew I must go back to school and try to get a master's degree so that I could go South and teach English in a College." The graduate programs in Chicago did not interest her, and it was not until she spoke to librarian Vivian Harsh at the George Cleveland Hall Branch of the Chicago Public Library that she first heard about a new, exciting graduate program in creative writing at the University of Iowa. Harsh was the first black professional librarian in the Chicago Public Library system. She served as head librarian at the Hall Branch, which was named for Dr. George Cleveland Hall, a physician and Chicago Public Library board member who pushed for this branch to open in a predominantly black middle-class neighborhood. The Hall Branch served as "a gathering place for young black writers and intellectuals," and Harsh invited black authors, including Margaret, to speak. Margaret recalls reading about the graduate program at Iowa in *Life* magazine:

> There was a big spread in *Life* magazine with pictures of Paul Engle and Norman Foerster and Dean George Dinsmore Stoddard plus pictures of Old Capitol and part of the Iowa City Campus. Altogether three or four, maybe five pages. There were also pictures of Grant Wood and Thomas Hart Benton advertising the same program in Art—and one in Theatre under Professor[s] Mabre and Longman. I sat down at once and wrote letters to Norman Foerster, Director of the School of Letters, and Paul Engle, Writers Workshop, State University of Iowa.

Margaret's letter was well received and encouraging; both Iowa professors (Foerster and Engle) told her to come to the university in early September and "if my work was good they would do everything they could to help me." The next step, then, like her trip to New

Women's Reading Group, Hall Branch, Chicago Public Library, 1940. Vivian Harsh is at the back on the left.

York, would be to save enough money for a train ticket. In addition, Margaret needed money to pay for her college diploma; she had to have it in order to send Iowa a copy of her college transcript. She was waiting for her final paycheck from the WPA; she hoped it would be enough.

> When I received my money I had fifty dollars clear money. I paid the twenty dollars to Northwestern and had my transcript sent to Iowa. I paid two weeks rent in advance for ten dollars. I bought ten dollars worth of groceries and I took the last ten dollars and bought a railroad ticket to Iowa City for four dollars and thirty-five or fifty cents.

Margaret recalls saying good-bye to Mercedes at the LaSalle Street Station. She was bound for the University of Iowa and a new adventure. Twenty-four years old, she writes, "I was not in the least afraid of what lay before me. I was too young to be cautious. All my life lay ahead of me. Only the past was dead."

5. Iowa

Writing "For My People"

Twice I have gone out to Iowa feeling that my life was over and each time
my life has blossomed in ways I could not even imagine. In Iowa things
got started. There was a foundation laid for everything that followed.
—*Margaret Walker, unpublished autobiography*

*M*argaret Walker left Chicago in September 1939 and took a train,
alone, to Iowa City, Iowa, to continue her education at the university
there. The University of Iowa's famed Iowa Writers' Workshop officially began in 1936, and it was to this new program that Margaret
was destined. When Margaret arrived, her first meeting was with
Norman Foerster, professor of English, and she recalls in her unpublished autobiography that upon hearing her name and seeing her
standing in front of him he "stared at me as if he could not believe
his ears." "You're Margaret Walker?" he asked, incredulously, and she
replied, "Yes, Sir, and I wrote you a letter which you answered and
here I am. And he stared again and then he said, 'Well, all I can say
is you surely write a good letter.' For a long while I was puzzled and
only after much reflection did I realize he did not expect a black person." Paul Engle, however, was not shocked by this petite, African
American young woman, and was determined that Margaret should
stay and would help her find the necessary financial aid.

Engle took Margaret to meet Dean George Dinsmore Stoddard,
who, along with Foerster and Engle, were all behind what Margaret
calls "a new experiment in Iowa in graduate education." At Iowa, a

new degree called an MFA, or Master of Fine
Arts, could be earned for a variety of creative
work:

> A creative person could write a book for a thesis
> in English, do an acting role in theatre, paint or
> sculpt in art or compose in music for a master's or
> a master of Fine Arts degree. This had just been
> announced and there were jobs and stipends,
> scholarships and fellowships to help support one.

Paul Engle, c. 1957.

Margaret feared she had arrived too late to re-
ceive financial aid, but Engle and Stoddard helped her find a job as a
research assistant, which was not an easy task. Margaret remembers
that "they had to search around for someone who not only needed a
research assistant but was willing to have a Negro, me."

Miss Luella Margaret Wright hired Margaret as her research assistant to help her with her articles for the journal of the Iowa State
Historical Society for thirty dollars per month. It was a start, but
not enough to cover room and board at Miss Frances Culbertson's
boardinghouse where Margaret had found a room. And, again, Paul
Engle saved the day, reminding Margaret of her Methodist heri-
tage, and it was to the Methodists that she turned for a loan. The
local Methodist church in Ames, Iowa, helped Margaret finance her
graduate education; they even took up a special collection, Margaret
recalls, and when she left Iowa with her master's degree, she proudly
stated in her autobiography, "[I] owed nobody a dime."

In Iowa Margaret found friends and instructors that inspired her
as she had in Chicago. Her roommate at Miss Culbertson's was artist Elizabeth Catlett, who was studying sculpture and painting with
artist Grant Wood, and whose thesis project was a stone sculpture
of a Negro mother and child. And she recalls having "remarkable
teachers":

> Austin Warren was one of the most brilliant men I ever sat un-
> der and he was that very year collaborating with René Wellek on
> *Theory of Literature.* Norman Foerster taught Literary Criticism, my

first encounter with the subject. Professor Thornton in American Civilization seemed genuinely interested in my Civil War novel as a research project. He gave me a list of books to read and told me what I should do to begin the research on what became *Jubilee*. I made my only A that year in American Civilization.

The most influential professor, however, was Paul Engle, who not only helped Margaret find the means to stay in Iowa, but also challenged her as a writer. Every week she met with Engle, and every week she remembers "constantly clash[ing] with sharp words." She writes, "I thought he was insulting and condescending to me. He thought I was rude and sharp and bitter, and above all, ungrateful." He insisted she diversify. The poems she had previously published, he said, "were [all] in the same vein" and that she "needed variety in tone and subject matter." Engle suggested she write some "Negro ballads," and even though she thought he was stereotyping her when he made that suggestion, she discovered that she enjoyed writing them and was good at it. Thus, despite their differences, Engle challenged Margaret and she was able to find a new poetic genre, expanding her range into a poetry collection that eventually became her master's thesis.

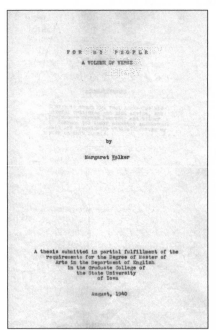

FOR MY PEOPLE
A VOLUME OF VERSE

by

Margaret Walker

A thesis submitted in partial fulfillment of the
requirements for the Degree of Master of
Arts in the Department of English
in the Graduate College of
the State University
of Iowa

August, 1940

Cover page for Margaret Walker's "For My People: A Volume of Verse." M.A. thesis, University of Iowa, 1940.

Margaret was focused on her thesis at the end of 1939 when, she writes, "the bottom dropped out." Marion contracted influenza and had to leave her job, and Mercedes left school for lack of money. Margaret traveled to Chicago to check on her sister, and when she returned her tuition for the second semester was due. The Methodist Church was able to pay fifty-two of the fifty-seven-dollar tuition, and when she asked her father for the remaining five dollars he replied that he did not have it. This stress was compounded by the publication of Richard Wright's novel *Native*

Son, which was a literary sensation. His success, the shortage of funds, and a third failed attempt to win the Yale Series of Younger Poets competition sent Margaret into a downward spiral and she went to speak to a psychiatrist.

It was a difficult time in Margaret's life, and she needed a break. She took the semester off to focus on her mental health and did not graduate with her friends; instead she typed dissertations to pay for her room and completed her degree during summer school. She recalls, "I passed [my exams] with flying colors . . .[and then] something wonderful happened. In July my manuscript came back [from the Yale Series of Younger Poets competition] but with it came a letter from Stephen Vincent Benét. It said:

Stephen Vincent Benét, 1919.

> Dear Miss Walker—
>
> I regret to inform you that your manuscript "For My People" has not been selected for inclusion in the Yale Series of Younger Poets. . . .
> It may interest you to know that "For My People" was one of the two or three manuscripts—out of fifty that came to me—which I considered up to the end. If you haven't placed it with another publisher next year I should be very glad to look at it again. I think you have an enormous amount of stuff and I think you are going places. The title poem, the poem called "Southern Song" and some of the Negro folk ballads are, to me, extraordinary work.

Even though *For My People* did not win the Yale prize, Margaret was encouraged by Benét's praise. She graduated from Iowa with her master's degree (1940) and found a teaching job at Livingstone College in Salisbury, North Carolina. She remembers her first paycheck for $135: "I sent thirty-five dollars to mama, opened a checking account, and bought clothes." She also recalls the professional opportunities that the president of Livingstone provided; the college offered to pay for Margaret to attend her first professional meeting, the annual College Language Association (CLA) meeting at Hampton

Margaret Walker, c. 1942.

Institute in Hampton, Virginia. Margaret recalls that the CLA was controlled "almost entirely by men," but she learned two important pieces of information at the conference: one, that her poem "For My People" had been published in *The Negro Caravan,* the landmark anthology of African American writing published in 1941; and two, that she was to be selected the next winner of the Yale Series of Younger Poets, the prize that had eluded her for years. She recalls hearing that she won from poet Owen Dodson and her stunned surprise. Her manuscript was still in her dresser drawer at home; she had not resubmitted it to Benét. However, in June the request for the manuscript came, and she quickly sent it. She writes, "In a matter of days

I received a telegram from Daddy saying, 'You won the Yale Award.
Letter from Benét follows.'"

In a 1982 interview with Claudia Tate, Margaret shares how she
believes Benét finally convinced the panel of judges to give her the
award:

> That year, 1942, was the last year Benét edited the Yale Younger Poet
> Series. I think he simply confronted his colleagues with the fact that
> if they wouldn't give the award to me, he wasn't going to name any-
> body else. In other words, I think he was telling them he was through
> with them if they didn't give it to me. After all, he had repeatedly said
> the piece was as near perfect as I could make it. I think he felt they
> were refusing purely on the basis of race. I didn't know how much the
> issue had gone back and forth between them until I went up there [to
> receive the award].

Livingstone College celebrated the success of its young faculty member, and Margaret intended to continue to teach at the school the
following year. However, when she returned to New Orleans for the
summer to visit her family, she discovered that her mother had accepted a job on her behalf because of the salary. Margaret recalls that
her mother felt she had to grab the two-hundred-dollar-per-month
teaching position at West Virginia State College "before somebody
else did." Therefore, Margaret joined the English Department at
West Virginia State College in the fall. She had never made so much
money in her life, but the substantial salary did not make the teaching situation less stressful. She could not find a permanent housing
situation, and she blames it on her race and gender:

> The night I arrived I had no place to go. The dean had leaned out of
> his bedroom window to tell the driver to take me to so-and-so's house
> for the time being. The next day they moved me to another place
> where I was clearly unwanted. After Christmas I moved into an apart-
> ment I expected to share with another young woman and found my-
> self in a threesome. . . . Next I moved in with a crazy woman. Finally
> the administration let me go where I had been told all year I could not
> stay, to a dormitory. Five places in one school year. I had had it! Had I
> been a man, no one would have dared move me around like that.

For My People, Yale Series
of Younger Poets Edition.

In addition, Margaret had to report to a very difficult head of the department. She describes her first staff meeting with Miss Lorene Kemp:

When I knocked on the door of the room where she was holding [the] first English staff meeting, she came to the door and when I asked— "Miss Kemp" she drew herself up and told me in a very frosty voice "I'm busy." When I asked "Is this the English meeting? I think I'm supposed to be here. My name is Margaret Walker," she dropped to half her height and became more effusive. "Oh, Miss Walker, I thought you were a student." I entered the room thinking, *"You don't talk to a dog that way."* I saw my colleagues smiling, smirking, and tittering.

Margaret and Miss Kemp's relationship never improved; in fact, it deteriorated further after *For My People* was published by Yale University Press and the college announced a book party. Margaret traveled to New York for events, and she had a whirlwind tour of readings and engagements. Stephen Vincent Benét demonstrated his belief in Margaret's talent by writing the foreword to the first edition of *For My People* himself. He praised her skill in writing all types of verse—sonnets, ballads, free verse—and summed up her work with the following observation:

> ... in whatever medium she is working, the note is true and unforced. There is a deep sincerity in all these poems—a sincerity at times disquieting. For this is what one American has found and seen—this is the song of her people, of her part of America. You cannot deny its honesty, you cannot deny its candor. And this is not far away or long ago—this is part of our nation, speaking.

Thus, 1942 would be a turning point in the life of Margaret Walker. In addition to her winning the Yale prize, the foreword by Benét jumpstarted Margaret's career. She tells friend and colleague Alferdteen Harrison about *For My People*'s "illustrious start" in a 1992 interview:

> Winning the Yale Award for Younger Poets was a distinction in itself. And when I went to New York to promote the book, I was invited to the New York Herald Tribune Book and Author Luncheon at the Hotel Astor where I read my poetry. That began my career as a lecturer. Everywhere I went and people heard me read my poetry, the word spread to others that I could read my poetry well. I have never lacked for engagements; I simply couldn't always fill them.

Richard K. Barksdale, author of the essay "Margaret Walker: Folk Orature and Historical Prophecy," noted that "[i]n 1942, when, at twenty-seven, she published her first volume of poems—*For My People*—she became one of the youngest Black writers to have published a volume of poetry in this country. . . . Moreover, when [this] volume won a poetry prize in 1942, Margaret Walker became the first Black woman in American literary history to be so honored in a prestigious national competition." Margaret's career was clearly on the rise in 1942, and she was focused and driven in both her teaching and oratory. However, 1942 would usher in one more positive surprise: Margaret would meet her future husband, Firnist James Alexander, when she least expected it.

6. *Writing* Jubilee

A Balancing Act

Long before *Jubilee* had a name, I was living with it and imagining its reality. Its genesis coincides with my childhood, its development grows out of a welter of raw experiences and careful research, and its final form emerged exactly one hundred years after its major events took place. Most of my life I have been involved with writing this story about my great-grandmother, and even if *Jubilee* were never considered an artistic or commercial success I would still be happy just to have finished it.

—Margaret Walker, "How I Wrote Jubilee*"*

In 1942, returning on a train from a reading, Margaret met the man she would eventually marry and with whom she would spend the next thirty-seven years: Firnist James Alexander, or "Alex." At the age of twenty-seven she had only had one serious relationship before meeting Alex. In a 1977 interview with Marcia Greenlee, Margaret revealed that she believes her mother discouraged amorous advances from suitors because she had seen too many of her siblings make unfortunate marriages, and she did not want her children to struggle as she had—marrying and having children before the age of twenty. For instance, when Margaret met a young man studying at the University of Chicago Theological Seminary while she was at Northwestern and he eventually proposed, she wrote her mother a letter asking her help in planning a wedding. She recalls her mother writing her "an awful letter [saying] that I was too young, although I was older than she was when she married. She was bitterly opposed to it."

Although Margaret felt that marriage to a minister would have been the right fit, as it was the only model she had ever known, she also reveals to Greenlee that accepting that proposal of marriage from the young Chicago minister would have been a mistake. Not for the reasons her mother cited, but because he was not willing to encourage and support her with her own career—he was looking for a helpmate. Despite their similar backgrounds and apparent compatibility, she realized later he was, in fact, all wrong for her:

> I felt that he was intelligent and sensitive and deeply religious and this would be just what I should do. Now I realize it would have been following the pattern of my family, which did not necessarily mean happiness for me. I guess I had many other-worldly notions that I was perhaps not as religious as I thought I was. I would have felt very cramped as a minister's wife. I thought I would have made a good minister's wife because that's all I'd ever known and seen. But that was one possibility that didn't work and now I'm very happy that it didn't.

She never fathomed, however, that she would find love and happiness with an uneducated military man.

Despite his good looks (Margaret says she "had never seen anybody who to me was more physically attractive and more magnetic"), Margaret fled when Alex first approached her on the train: "I was against the war and bitterly opposed soldiers . . . so when he tried to strike up an acquaintance—he made a pass at me from the train

Firnist James Alexander's draft card. Alex enlisted
September 5, 1942.

Margaret Walker at Yaddo, an artists' retreat in Saratoga Springs, New York, 1943. Margaret Walker is seated second from the left. Author Carson McCullers is seated second from right, and Langston Hughes is standing, far right.

I was about to board—I ran." But he was not deterred. She recalls that "[b]y the time I got myself settled and got my breath and my luggage—I looked around and he was standing over me smiling." He refused to be ignored and Margaret remembers his passionate, persuasive opening speech: "[H]e said something about just because they had no future a soldier was a person just like anybody else and why should they be treated like scum, you know, like dirt under your feet. And why would I refuse even to let him sit down and speak to me. [W]ho was I? [S]ome holy sanctified and sanctimonious woman who was going around preaching?"

Margaret relented and permitted this handsome young soldier to sit beside her, and discovered, as she had with Richard Wright, that intelligence cannot be measured by years of academia. Alex may have lacked a high school diploma, but Margaret says to Greenlee that "I could not tell at the time that he wasn't as well educated as the young people I had already begun to teach. He spoke and read and wrote as well as the average college student." They married in June the following year, and their marriage, Margaret believes, lasted because it was based on "honesty, frankness [and] truth." On the train Alex spoke his mind, and Margaret says that in their thirty-seven years of marriage, "I don't think I have ever really caught my husband in a lie." Margaret and Alex began their married life in 1943 in High Point, North Carolina, and Margaret's good fortune continued. In addition to teaching, she published "Growing Out of Shadow" in *Common Ground*, and was selected to attend Yaddo, an artists' retreat in Saratoga Springs, New York. Encouraged by Langston Hughes, who was the first African American to attend in 1942, Margaret applied and was accepted the following year. Margaret, the first African American woman to attend Yaddo, joined distinguished company at the artists' community in upstate New York. In addition to Hughes, who attended a second year, she worked alongside writers Carson McCullers and Jean Stafford. Margaret also met Phyllis Moir of the National Artists and Concert Corporation in New York City in 1943, who had heard Margaret read her poetry at a luncheon and was duly impressed. She invited Margaret to her home on Fifth Avenue and told the aspiring writer: "I would like to help you let the rest of the nation hear your voice." She guaranteed Margaret a significant pay increase and more time to write. Margaret quickly accepted Ms. Moir's offer, and although she and Alex continued to live in North Carolina, Margaret began a lecture and reading tour over the next five years with the National Artists and Concert Corporation for a salary three times as much as she was making teaching.

In 1944 Margaret earned another literary reward: she received a Rosenwald Fellowship, which allowed her to continue doing research on *Jubilee*. The Julius Rosenwald Fund Fellowship Program "awarded grants to hundreds of African American writers, educators, artists and scholars, as well as southern whites with interests in race relations" between 1928 and 1948. Although the birth of her first child, a daughter, Marion (who was named in honor of her mother and who, like both her mother and grandparents, was born in July) delayed the start of her return to her research, the fellowship allowed Margaret to make an exciting discovery:

> At that time I was seeking information about free Negroes in Georgia. . . . Carter G. Woodson had written a book on *The Heads of Free Negro Families* in 1830, and among those listed was a family named Ware—the name of my maternal great grand-mother. I found that

this family might have originated on the Atlantic Coast, in Virginia or the Carolinas. At least they had made early appearances there and may have emigrated to America from the West Indies. Then, as I was reading materials from the congressional investigations of the Ku Klux Klan, I found that one of the victims was an artisan named Ware, who was living in a county adjacent to my story's location. I could not swear that Randall Ware was a member of our family, but one could make a good, educated guess that he was.

This discovery and Margaret's desire to learn about her family is all the more significant as her grandmother, Elvira Ware Dozier, who had raised her along with her parents and told her the stories which became the basis of *Jubilee*, died. Now that her grandmother was no longer available as a source, it was up to Margaret to piece together and document the story of her family.

Margaret's research would be interrupted again with the birth of her second child, Firnist James Alexander, Jr. With a two-year-old and an infant, Margaret had time for little else but taking care of her children. However, in 1947, a speaking engagement brought her to Albany, Georgia, which was located in the vicinity of Dawson, the birthplace of her grandmother and setting of *Jubilee*. She decided to make the trip to Dawson even though she knew no family was there, and see if she could learn anything about the Wares:

> I went into the colored community and began inquiring about my great-grandparents. I found a man who remembered my great-grandfather, Randall Ware. He said [Ware] had lived into his nineties, and had died about 1925. If I wished, the man said, he would show me Ware's smithy, his grist mill, and his homeplace. All this was completely astonishing to me, since I had never known much about Randall Ware except my grandmother's remarks that he was a freeman from birth, that he was a smith who owned his own smithy, that he could read and write, and that he was a rich man. Now I was thrilled to see the smithy and his anvil, his grist mill, and his gingerbread house.

The success of this trip enabled Margaret to finally imagine the structure of her family saga: "For the first time I clearly envisioned the development of a folk novel, and prepared an outline of incidents and general chapter headings. I knew that the center of my story was Vyry [the female protagonist based on Margaret's great-grandmother] and that the book should end with Randall Ware's return."

However, again Margaret had to put the novel aside and focus on family and making ends meet. Her third child, Sigismund Constantine, was born July 26, 1949, and with three children under the age of six, Margaret returned to full-time teaching. She joined the English Department of Jackson State College in Jackson, Mississippi, in the fall, and although this educational institution was to be her academic home for the next thirty years, she recalls a difficult start there:

Margaret Walker's great-grandmother, Margaret Duggans Ware Brown.

In September 1949, when I began teaching in Jackson, Mississippi, I was married and the mother of three children. My youngest was nine weeks old the day I began. . . . [M]embers of the administration kept saying they were honored to have me, until I moved my family and furniture. They saw that my husband was sick and disabled from the war, that I had three children under six years of age, [and] that I was poor and had to work. I was no longer their honored poet, but a defenseless Black woman to be harassed.

Despite what Margaret perceived as the administration's ungracious attitude, she taught her classes and performed additional time-consuming tasks that were asked of her, such as organizing literary festivals, writing occasional poems, and producing pageants. As with "The Golden Whistle," the opera that Margaret had directed on her ninth birthday, she would bring and direct significant literary events at Jackson State during her thirty-year career. Her husband, Alex, was a great support as he only worked part-time due to a medical disability and was able to help with the children.

Margaret Walker organized Jackson State's 75th Jubilee Anniversary in October 1952 and invited a stellar group of writers to commemorate the occasion. Back row: Arna Wendell Bontemps, Melvin B. Tolson, President Jacob L. Reddix, Owen Dodson, and Robert C. Hayden. Front row: Sterling Allen Brown, Ruth Roseman Dease, Margaret Walker, and Langston Hughes.

In 1953, Margaret was awarded a Ford Fellowship, which provided her with the funds to take time off from teaching for fifteen months and return to her research on *Jubilee*. Sadly, however, her father died at the same time she received the Ford prize. Returning from his funeral in New Orleans, though, took her through Greenville, Alabama, and she decided to again look for family and trace their path from Greenville to Dawson. In her essay "How I Wrote *Jubilee*," written in 1972, Margaret describes what she found:

In Greenville, I found my grandmother's youngest, and last-surviving, sister, who gave me a picture of my great-grandmother, corroborated my grandmother's account, and let me see the family Bible and the chest my great-grandmother had carried from the plantation. Later, as we traveled through the Georgia environs of what was my lost plantation, we found an antebellum home near Bainbridge, Georgia, with the square pillars and the separated kitchen-house as described in the story. The lady of the house was kind enough to let me come in and look through her place.

The Ford Fellowship also allowed Margaret to leave Jackson and travel with her family to the University of North Carolina first and then Yale to conduct research. She moved her husband and three young children to Durham, North Carolina, and while the children were in school, Alex would drive Margaret to the neighboring city of Chapel Hill to do research at the Southern Historical Collection and "[delve] into the Nelson Tift papers, a collection of account books, diaries, letters, bills of sale, and other personal papers of a wealthy white Georgia planter who had lived in the environs of my story during antebellum days." Margaret used several items from the Tift collection in her novel, such as "the letter Grimes wrote the master when the slaves had broken into the smokehouse, the conversation among the planters at Marse John's dinner party, and information concerning the two women condemned to hang for the murder of their master and his mother."

Another source of valuable information found in North Carolina was the slave narratives Margaret discovered in the Martin Collection at North Carolina College (later North Carolina Central University). In "How I Wrote *Jubilee*," Margaret discusses the importance of these narratives to her research:

> These slave narratives only further corroborated the most valuable slave narrative of all, the living account of my great-grandmother, which had been transmitted to me by her own daughter. I knew then that I had a precious, almost priceless, living document of my own. There are hundreds of these stories, most of them not written, but many of them recorded for posterity. These written accounts tell of the brutalizing and dehumanizing practices of human slavery. They recount such atrocities as branding, whipping, killing, and mutilating slaves. They are sometimes written in the form of letters to former masters, sometimes as autobiographical sketches, and some—like that of Frederick Douglass—have become classics. And all of them contain crucial information on slavery from the mouth of the slave.

After North Carolina, the family traveled to New Haven, Connecticut, where Yale University is located, and Margaret spent a semester revising *Jubilee* under the supervision of Professor Holmes Pearson. She made progress, but she recalls leaving Yale with

The Walker children (left to right): Margaret, Sigismund, Firnist, Jr., and Marion.

"Professor Pearson's criticism in my ears: 'You are telling the story, but it does not come alive.'"

The funds available from the Ford Fellowship now depleted, the Walkers returned to Mississippi, and Margaret began teaching again at Jackson State in September 1954. Their fourth child and second daughter, Margaret Elvira, was born in June, and when they returned to Jackson Margaret was forced to put away her manuscript and focus on family. They needed a house and Alex would require multiple surgeries over the next seven years. Margaret writes that "[f]rom 1955 until 1962 I published nothing . . . but nothing prevented my reading piles of books—nights, Sundays, and holidays." She became an expert on the Civil War and Reconstruction, reading authors Francis Butter Simkins, W. E. B. Du Bois, Benjamin Quarles, and Charles Wesley. She even lectured on the war in her classes. Steeped in all this reading and research, she knew it was time to take her *Jubilee* manuscript out once again. And in the summer of 1961 she took it back to the teacher and to the school where she had learned the most about writing—Paul Engle at the University of Iowa.

7. *Finishing* Jubilee

Back to Iowa

People ask me how I find time to write, with a family and a teaching
job. I don't. That is one reason I was so long with *Jubilee*. A writer needs
time to write a certain number of hours every day. This is particularly
true with prose fiction and absolutely necessary with the novel. . . . It is
humanly impossible for a woman who is a wife and mother to work on
a regular teaching job and write. Weekends and nights and vacations
are all right for reading, but not enough for writing.
—*Margaret Walker, "How I Wrote* Jubilee"

In the summer of 1961, Margaret returned to Iowa looking for help
with her novel. Twenty-two years earlier, when she had come to Iowa
the first time to pursue her MFA, she was alone; this time she arrived with her two youngest children in tow, ages six and eleven. Even
though much time had passed and her circumstances had changed
greatly, Margaret knew that in Iowa she could not only find the guid-
ance and support she needed to finish *Jubilee*, but she also could earn
the highest academic degree in her field: her doctorate in English.
And, again, it was Paul Engle, her former advisor, who helped her
formulate a plan to not only complete her Ph.D. in English but to
use her novel as her dissertation. Margaret recalls in her essay "How I
Wrote *Jubilee*," "Suddenly all the pieces of my life seemed to be falling
into place and there was hope for the consolidation of the gains of all
the years."

Margaret spent the eight weeks of the summer of 1961 in a fiction
workshop with Professor Verlin Cassill, a prolific novelist and fellow

graduate of the Iowa MFA program. Margaret describes the eight-week workshop as "painful":

> My first short pieces did not please him at all, but when I showed him the much-revised first chapter of *Jubilee*, to my great surprise he gave it his complete approval. Meanwhile he had taught me how to read the masters of fiction, such as Chekhov, in order to learn how they put their material together. Cassill had not only put his finger on the problem, but he showed me how to dramatize my material and make it come alive. I had never had any trouble with dialogue, but now under his tutelage I was learning how to do close critical reading, and how to make character charts, establish relationships, and control the language more powerfully and effectively.

She returned to Jackson State at the end of the summer, but a year later realized that her dissertation would never be completed while she was teaching full-time. Margaret began a two-year leave of absence from Jackson State in the fall of 1962. She found a place to live with Alma B. Hovey, a retired Iowa English professor, who offered much more than a place to eat and sleep:

> Alma . . . was perpetually serene, . . . optimistic, and encouraging. Something of her spirit seemed contagious. "One thing at a time" was her first admonition, and finally I took it so seriously that we reached the point where she actually had to prod me through those awful Latin translations. Regularly she insisted on my drinking a cup of coffee in the morning before facing the Iowa weather and stopping in the afternoon to relax over a cup of hot tea. I found myself in the house of a friend.

Margaret recalls in a 1982 interview with John Griffin Jones that Iowa provided a refuge during a most difficult time at Jackson State. She stayed in Iowa for three years during the early 1960s because she did not want to take sides when lines were drawn for battle over segregation:

> I found myself in an untenable position in the early sixties. My students were in revolt, and the [Jackson State] administration was

holding the line for segregation on orders of the powers that be—
shall we say, the establishment. And like most of the teachers, I was
called in and asked whether I was on the side of the students or on
the side of the administration. And I said I couldn't take either side. If
I sided with my students against the administration, I wouldn't have
a job; and if I sided with the administration against the students, I
wouldn't have anybody to teach, and I wouldn't be able to do that
either. So I went to school. . . . in '61 I went out to Iowa, and I came
back in the state through a hellish year, '61 and '62, but the fall of '62
I was in Iowa and I stayed there three years. And I came back, and
it was still going on. But I was gone the most violent year of all. 1963
was the most violent year.

Margaret is referring first to the murder that occurred on the same
street as her own home in Jackson. Her neighbor and friend, Medgar
Evers, a civil rights activist, was assassinated in the driveway of his
home on Guynes Street on June 12. She also tells John Griffin Jones
that she is referring to the other events of that violent year: "Kennedy
was killed, the march on Washington, the children bombed in the
church in Birmingham—it was a violent year, it was a horrible year."
Even though she was in Iowa at the time, Evers's murder and these

Neighborhood children in front of Medgar Evers's house on Guynes Street,
Jackson, Mississippi.

other brutal incidents spurred Margaret to write a number of civil rights poems. These poems eventually became *Prophets for a New Day*, which was published in 1970.

The title, *Prophets for a New Day*, refers to the majority of poems in the collection that equate civil rights leaders with biblical prophets of the past. The blending of Margaret's religious upbringing with her poetic talents is dramatically displayed in these powerful poems. For instance, "Micah," the poem composed in honor of Medgar Evers, draws the analogy between the biblical prophet and the young civil rights advocate in the opening lines:

> *Micah was a young man of the people*
> *Who came up from the streets of Mississippi*
> *And cried out his Vision to his people;*
> *Who stood fearless before the waiting throng*
> *Like an astronaut shooting into space.*
> *Micah was a man who spoke against Oppression (1–6)*

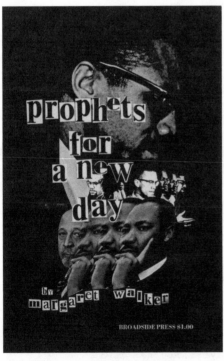

Cover of *Prophets for a New Day.*

Martin Luther King, Jr., is compared both to Moses in "At the Lincoln Monument in Washington August 28, 1963" and the prophet Amos when Margaret writes in a poem entitled "Amos—1963," "Amos is our Shepherd standing in the Shadow of our God / Tending his flocks all over the hills of Albany / And the seething streets of Selma and of bitter Birmingham" (18–20) and in a second poem entitled "Amos (Postscript—1968)" when she describes King as "a man of peace for the people / Amos is a Prophet of the Lord / Amos speaks through Eternity / The glorious Word of the Lord!" (7–10).

Margaret also writes poems directed to other heroes and martyrs of the civil rights movement: the leaders of the Greensboro, North Carolina, sit-ins; Nat Turner, Gabriel Prosser, Denmark Vesey, and John Brown; Malcolm X; and Andrew Goodman, Michael Schwerner, and James Chaney, the three civil rights workers murdered in Philadelphia, Mississippi, in June 1964. Poems in the collection are also composed about civil war battlegrounds, such as Jackson and Birmingham, cities where Margaret has lived and is living, and she emotionally expresses the tension between the cities' racial unrest and natural beauty in powerfully raw first-person narrative:

Medgar Evers.

City of tense and stricken faces . . .
City of barbed wire stockades, . . .
Hauling my people in garbage trucks,
Fenced in by new white police billies,
Fist cuffs and red-necked brothers of Hate Legions . . .
City of tree-lined, wide, white avenues
And black alleys of filthy rendezvous;
City of flowers: of new red zinnias
And oriental poppies and double-ruffled petunias . . .
City of stooges and flunkeys, pimps and prostitutes,
Bar-flies and railroad-station freaks; . . .
I give you my heart, Southern City
For you are my blood and dust of my flesh,
You are the harbor of my ship of hope, . . .
I give you my brimming heart, Southern City
For my eyes are full and no tears cry
And my throat is dusty and dry.

(From "Jackson, Mississippi")

In 1964 Margaret's focus shifted constantly between her family, the civil rights atrocities happening in her home state and around the country, and completing her Ph.D. and novel *Jubilee*. She successfully passed her written and oral exams in fall 1964, the penultimate requirement for earning her doctorate in English; all that was left now was finishing her Civil War novel. The pressure to finish the first draft of the manuscript was overwhelming because Margaret's dissertation adviser, Verlin Cassill, was threatening to leave Iowa. Miss Hovey saved the day again, providing not only much-needed support but a very important resource, a book of songs from one hundred years ago that contained "Civil War songs, Stephen Foster songs, Negro Folk songs—including spirituals, work songs, popular tunes, and even minstrel songs and favorites I had heard my grandmother say that my great-grandmother had sung" that Margaret used as epigraphs in the novel. She also offered to proofread Margaret's pages:

> . . . I was sick with apprehension and fear over the possible departure of my key faculty reader. But just as I thought it would drive me to physical illness, Miss Hovey decided that she would read each page I wrote. Then we discussed it in terms of the whole story and she commented and made suggestions, either approving or disagreeing. That saved the day. By February 22, 1965, I had completed the second section, that terrible Civil War—which my husband declared he had been fighting all the twenty-odd years of our marriage.

And two months later Margaret finally completed the first draft of *Jubilee*. However, she says in "How I Wrote *Jubilee*," that even though completing the first draft was a huge accomplishment, it was just the beginning: "[T]he end of the first draft is not by any means the end of the writing. I believe that writing is nine-tenths rewriting. . . . I always write too much and too easily and therefore I must always cut, cut, cut and revise many times. A first draft is only the beginning."

A period of furious revising began because Margaret was intent on completing the novel and graduating with her Ph.D. in June. She accomplished her goal, and in June 1965 not only received her degree but returned to Jackson State with a book contract in hand from Houghton Mifflin. *Jubilee* finally was published on September 25,

First edition of *Jubilee* in window of Elson's Department Store.

1966, and won the prestigious Houghton Mifflin Literary Award, an award that has launched many American writers' careers, including Philip Roth's. Initial reviews of the novel, however, were mixed: Wilma Dykeman, writing for the *New York Times Book Review*, called the novel "ambitious" but "uneven"; Arthur Chapman of *The Saturday Review* complimented Walker's "fidelity to fact and detail"; and Henrietta Buckmaster in *The Christian Science Monitor* focused on Walker's protagonist, Vyry, who "suffered one outrage after the other and yet emerged with a humility and moral fortitude that reflected a spiritual wholeness." For Margaret, the critics could say what they wanted; after thirty years she was finished, and she remarked that "even if *Jubilee* were never considered an artistic or commercial success I would still be happy just to have finished it."

The achievement of *Jubilee* cannot be overstated; it is, according to Jacqueline Miller Carmichael, "one of the first novels to present the nineteenth-century African American historical experience in the South from a black and female point of view." As stated earlier, it traces the life of a single slave woman, Vyry, whose life is based on Margaret's great-grandmother, Margaret Duggans Ware Brown, from "the slave cabin to the 'Big House,' and from slavery to freedom." Walker organizes the novel into three sections: the antebellum era, the Civil War, and Reconstruction. After the enormous amount of research undertaken in order to write the novel, Margaret Walker asks the obvious question in her essay "How I Wrote *Jubilee*": "How much of *Jubilee* is fiction and how much fact?" And she supplies the answer:

> When you have lived with a story as long as I have with this one, it is difficult sometimes to separate the two, but let us say that the basic skeleton of the story is factually true and authentic. Imagination has worked with this factual material, however, for a very long time. The entire story follows a plot line of historical incidents from the first chapter until the last: the journeys, the Big Road, the violence, the battles, the places Vyry and Innis lived and the reasons they moved.
>
> I had very little to go on, however, with my white characters, and many of them are composites. The middle section of the story is my most highly imagined section, since I had only fragments that had to be pieced together. The entire white family is obviously symbolic of the Confederate South, from the death of the master, who was sure the Union didn't have a leg to stand on, until the death of the mistress in the face of the complete collapse of the Confederacy. The young master and Lillian are both part of this larger symbol.

Jacqueline Miller Carmichael also notes how the ending of the novel brings the reader right into the present—the 1960s: "The ending of *Jubilee* suggests a connection between the events the novel has described during Reconstruction and the civil rights movement of the 1960s. The narrative ends on a train bound for Selma. As Jim and his father [Randall Ware] board the train, the conductor announces the segregated seating order—colored up front and whites in the rear." Margaret Walker may have written a Civil War novel, but it resonates, as Carmichael points out, and cannot be disconnected from the time in which she wrote it.

8. Returning Home

Establishing the Institute for the Study of the History, Life, and Culture of Black People

---

> Our greatest weapon is the word. The black scholar is a man of thought and action who thinks for his people and acts with them.
> —*Margaret Walker, "The Challenge of the 1970s to the Black Scholar"*

Jubilee was finally published, but it did not make Margaret Walker a rich woman. It brought her literary fame: in addition to the Houghton Mifflin Award, Walker was presented with the Mable Carney Student National Education Association plaque for scholar-teacher of the year and the Alpha Kappa Alpha Sorority Citation for Advancement of Knowledge. The following year, 1967, she sold the paperback rights to Bantam, and the folk novel has never gone out of print. Walker jokingly remarked to friend and Jackson State colleague Dr. Alferdteen Harrison that "the royalty checks were wonderful Christmas presents," but that she has never gotten rich from her novel. In an interview with Kay Bonetti in 1991, Walker recounts how in 1966 she was still facing obstacles in promoting *Jubilee*:

> My southern salesman said if I had been a white woman writing that book I would be a rich woman. He went to a bookstore in Atlanta to get them to have an autograph party and when they discovered I was black, they told him no. He came to one of the church bookstores in Jackson, I think Southern Baptist, and although I had been a regular customer and had bought many, many books, they refused to have the book autographed in their store. But a big department store that

Margaret Walker signing copies of *Jubilee*. From left to right is Sarah Dilworth Lang, Dr. Mabel Pittman Middleton, Paula Pittman, and Inez Morris Chambers, all colleagues of Margaret Walker in the English department at Jackson State.

Jackson State celebrated the publication of *Jubilee*. Here Margaret Walker is giving Jackson State University President Jacob L. Reddix a copy of the newly published novel. Seated left is Violet Williams and seated right is Daisy Reddix. A picture of Margaret Walker's great-grandmother, Margaret Duggans Ware Brown, is displayed on the wall in the background.

has stores over Louisiana and Alabama gave me a wonderful auto-graph signing. The woman in that store said she sold more [copies of *Jubilee*] than she had sold of any book in twenty years.

In the same interview Bonetti asked Margaret if she knew who was buying the book—blacks or whites? And Walker replied, both: "Black and white. People in the South ate up that book quickly."

The publication of *Jubilee* did not mean that Margaret was idle; on the contrary, she turned her attention back to teaching and to Jackson State, where she made historic contributions to the university that would place her in the forefront of scholarship and learning. In 1968 Margaret established the Institute for the Study of the History, Life, and Culture of Black People, one of the first black studies programs in the country. Initially the institute was simply a room with a desk and a telephone, but its formation was extremely significant. It put Margaret "at the forefront of a nascent Black Studies movement." A black revolution was happening all across the country, with pro-tests at institutions such as San Francisco State, Northwestern, Harvard, and the City University of New York demanding the cre-ation of black studies departments, increases in black student enrollment, and more finan-cial aid for minority students. In her book *The Black Revolution on Campus*, Martha Biondi traces the origins of this black revolution, but surprisingly she does not mention Margaret

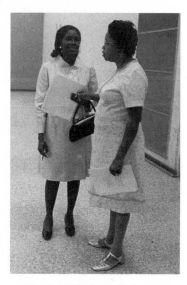

Margaret Walker with Alleane Currie, her assistant at the institute, in the Jacob L. Reddix Campus Union Building, Jackson State University, November 1973.

Walker once. Reviewer Julianne Malveaux also noted the lack of photos of any women who were instrumental in the struggle from 1968 to 1973:

Unfortunately Biondi—or her publisher—reinforces gender bias with the photos that are included in the book. Only one features a black woman, Eva Jefferson (later Eva Jefferson Patterson) of

Northwestern University, speaking at a rally in Chicago. Perhaps no other pictures were available, but it would have been useful to see some pictures of the "women behind the scenes" who are often rendered invisible.

Walker was hardly invisible; with the publication of *Jubilee* in 1966 and the establishment of the institute in 1968, she was very much on the frontlines of the revolution. She delivered the keynote address at the opening of the institute entitled "Critical Approaches to the Study of African American Literature," explicitly stating what she saw as the "controversial issues" confronting new students and scholars of African American literature. She raises important questions that she insisted had to be answered before moving forward:

> Not the least of these is the name given to the literature. Having begun as Negro literature, is it Afro-American literature, Black literature, or African American literature? Why not American literature? What is the historical context in which the literature should be read? Must it be approached from the sociological or ideological viewpoint rather than always from the critical imperative of analysis and synthesis? Is there a separate and distinctly black American tradition or African American tradition as distinguished from an Anglo-American or Anglo-Saxon tradition? Does this literature pose different aesthetic problems for the creative artist and critic from any other literature? Do black writers develop their literature from a different kind of ethos and mythological background than the white writer? Which world does this literature represent and why?

What Walker is providing is the blueprint for her institute and all other future black studies departments—the questions scholars must answer as they proceed further in their quest to establish their own centers of learning.

The Institute for the Study of the History, Life, and Culture of Black People, now known as the Margaret Walker Alexander National Research Center, is "dedicated to the preservation, interpretation, and dissemination of African-American history and culture." In the early days of the institute, Margaret accomplished this mission by going out on the road and speaking at meetings and conferences all over the country. The same year she founded the institute, she published "Religion, Poetry, and History: Foundations for a New Educational System" in *Vital Speeches of the Day*, calling for a new educational system out of the black protest movement:

> Our young people seem to be seething in a boiling caldron of discontent. Like the youth of every generation, they want to know, and they demand to be heard. Like youth in every age, they are the vanguard of our revolutionary age. They are the natural leaders of revolution, whether that revolution be of race, class or caste; whether it is sexual or academic; whether it is political or intellectual. Today, the revolution we are witnessing encompasses all of these . . . this new educational system must not be one of racial exclusion, or this will become another face for racism. This learning must be all-inclusive.

Margaret found herself in the heart of the revolution when her own institution, Jackson State, experienced violence on its campus. Ten days after the massacre at Kent State, two young men lost their lives on the Jackson campus. Jackson State students, like other college students across the country, had been protesting the United States' role in the Vietnam War. In addition, students at Jackson State were concerned with issues of relevance to historically black colleges such as matters of curriculum and course offerings. They also were fed up with harassment and intimidation by white motorists traveling on Lynch Street, "a major thoroughfare that divided the campus and linked West Jackson to downtown." It all came to a head on May 15, 1970,

> [w]hen Jackson police and Mississippi Highway Patrol officers suppressed student unrest with intense gunfire. Philip Lafayette Gibbs, 21, a junior pre-law major, and James Earl Green, a Jim Hill High School senior, were killed. Many students were injured, 12 by gunfire. A dormitory was riddled by 460 rounds, some holes still visible today. Law enforcement had massed at the college to subdue students protesting harassment from the whites driving through campus, police intimidation and the recent killing of four student demonstrators at Kent State University by the Ohio National Guard.

Margaret, understandably, was shocked and saddened by this event, and, as she had been inspired to do in the past, she wrote a poem about the tragedy entitled "Jackson State, May 15, 1970." The last three stanzas place readers right in the heart of the violence:

> *Shotguns, high-powered rifles crackling in the night*
> *   splattering glass and blood; screams cutting air with*
> *   death and fright; ambulances and sirens wailing;*
> *   streets covered with casings from their guns—highway*
> *   patrolmen's guns. . . .*
> *Death came and took our frozen young, our finest*
> *   flowers, our black-eyed-susan boys and men, and*
> *   wounded dozens more: women crouching in vain*
> *   behind the broken window pane, lying along*
> *   stairs, faces caricatured into spasms of*
> *   despair.*
> *Now all may see their faces in a marble monument, and*
> *   walk this plaza where they died in vain; but we will not*
> *   forget, for nothing is the same; never ever be the same*
> *   since that blue-reddened night.*

On August 13, 1970, Margaret was invited to testify about that tragic day at Jackson State before the President's Commission on Campus Unrest, and she recalls that "painful duty" in her remarks in a speech on the two-year anniversary of the event. She shared in this speech, which was later published as an essay, that in her testimony she "expressed the personal belief that this act of violence perpetuated against our people and our institution was an overt act of repression indicative of national repression and the direct results of racism and the widening of the war in Asia." Her testimony sparked outrage, and she recalled she received "a number of pieces of hate mail." She did not back down, however, and she told her audience, colleagues and students at Jackson State, that the fight was not over and they must recognize the role they played in the struggle. She directed her concluding remarks to the students themselves: "Your service is needed in your communities. . . . I challenge you to remember what happened on this campus two years ago. Remember and think again.

Jackson State massacre plaque.

Ask yourself, and remember. On pain of your own death—do not dare to forget."

In another important essay published in 1972, "Agenda for Action: Black Arts and Letters," first delivered as a speech at the Black Academy's Conference to Assess the State of Black Arts and Letters in the United States, which met in Chicago in 1972, Margaret reflected on the 1960s as she looked toward the future and the brand-new field of black studies:

> We can be eternally grateful for the revolutionary decade of the 1960s for a cultural reawakening to the worth of our heritage and the great potential of our people's destiny. What we inherit from the civil rights movement and the black revolution of racial consciousness are gems of inestimable worth. What have these social events done for us? They have given us renewed pride and dignity and a greater sense of mind and spirit. For we no longer possess a mass slave mentality.

Walker challenged the Black Academy to be an organization that "means more than a list of distinguished names. It should mean a bulwark of strength, to nourish both the old and the new—the

Margaret Walker with sculptor Elizabeth Catlett's bust of Phillis Wheatley.
Photograph © Roy Lewis Photography.

Margaret Walker, front and center, at the Phillis Wheatley Poetry Festival.
From left to right are Mari Evans, Sonia Sanchez, and June Jordan.
Photograph © Roy Lewis Photography.

established as well as the young black artists who are coming on."
She reiterated her desire for changes in the college curriculum in another essay written in 1972, "Humanities with a Black Focus," when
she called "teaching European art, music, literature, and Western civilization exclusively" at historically black colleges "a crime against . . .
black humanity." "World literature," she said, "begins with the ancient
Egyptian *Book of the Dead* which predates all the epics of Homer and

Virgil and obviously influences the Rhadamanthus legend from the beginning of recorded literature to Ralph Ellison's *Invisible Man.*" Margaret not only called for change; she made change at her own institution, Jackson State. After a two-year sabbatical from the campus that allowed her to work on book projects, conduct seminars at various institutions, and deliver speeches, Margaret returned home with an idea that, according to biographer Maryemma Graham, "help[ed] inaugurate the black women's literary renaissance." Margaret describes how she conceived the idea for the Phillis Wheatley Poetry Festival in her essay "Phillis Wheatley and Black Women Writers, 1773–1973":

> In October of 1972, I was on my way by train to Dayton, Ohio, for the centennial celebration of Paul Laurence Dunbar. I rode the train from Jackson to Effingham, Illinois, and would have to spend a day's layover before taking the "Spur" to Dayton. There in the Holiday Inn, I conceived the idea of a Phillis Wheatley Poetry Festival to be celebrated in 1973 on the bicentennial occasion of the first book published by an American woman. Dunbar was one hundred years old in 1972. Mary McLeod Bethune, the great educator and founder of Bethune-Cookman College [now University] . . . would be one hundred years old in 1975. What else would be more fitting in 1973?

A year later the festival was a reality, and twenty-six "outstanding black women" were invited to the campus of Jackson State to celebrate the bicentennial of the publication of Phillis Wheatley's *Poems on Various Subjects, Religious and Moral.* Wheatley's book was, according to Margaret Walker, "the first known book published by a black in America."

The list of guests was impressive. Among those invited and attending were Marion Alexander, Lucille Clifton, Mari Evans, Sarah Webster Fabio, Nikki Giovanni, Audre Lorde, June Jordan, Sonia Sanchez, and Alice Walker. Margaret recalled three events from the festival that made it especially significant:

> Nikki Giovanni, "the black princess of poetry" in the 1960s, gave a concert reading backed by a gospel choir from nearby Tougaloo College; the late Sarah Webster Fabio gave a reading accompanied by a family

Nikki Giovanni backed by Tougaloo College gospel choir. Photograph © Roy Lewis Photography.

jazz trio with a solo dancer and vocal soloist; and Alice Walker wrote a special piece for the festival, "In Search of Our Mothers' Gardens." That piece, which would appear in *MS Magazine* in 1974, has now become a classic. Every woman poet present at the festival had published at least one book of poetry, but several went on to distinguish themselves in the field of poetry and fiction, including Alice Walker, June Jordan, and Audre Lord. Now, looking back twenty years later, I realize how historic that occasion was. If Phillis Wheatley had only known what she had started.

Nineteen hundred seventy-three continued to be a productive year for Margaret. In addition to the accomplishment of the festival, she published another book of poems, *October Journey*, a collection described by Eleanor Traylor as both "autobiographical and occasional." Joyce Pettis groups *October Journey* with *Jubilee* and *Prophets for a New Day*, and says all three works mark "the beginning of a second phase of Walker's career, for these publications located her amidst a younger generation of writers," writers such as Alice Walker and Sonia Sanchez, with whom she was now connected through the Phillis Wheatley celebration.

Phillis Wheatley Poetry Festival participants. From left to right: Margaret Goss Burroughs, Marion Alexander, June Jordan, Dorothy Porter, Audre Lorde, Mari Evans, Malaika Wangara, Etta Moten Barnett, Paula Giddings, Alice Walker, Doris Saunders, Gloria Oden, Margaret Danner, Linda Brown Bragg, and Carole Gregory Clemmons. Photograph © Roy Lewis Photography.

Many poems in *October Journey* had been published previously; the collection spans from 1934 to 1972. Margaret described the title poem, which is considered by many scholars as the standout of the collection, in the preface to her poetry collection published in 1989, *This Is My Century: New and Collected Poems*:

> I wrote "October Journey," a poem that has multiple meanings in my life, in 1943 after a few weeks at Yaddo, where I wrote the ballad "Harriet Tubman." I was actually making the journey South in October, and "October Journey" expresses my emotions at that time. [It was also significant because] I met my husband in October . . .

Other notable poems in *October Journey* include the long "Epitaph for My Father"; the ballad "Harriet Tubman"; a beautiful sonnet, "Dear Are the Names that Charmed Me in My Youth"; occasional poems dedicated to noteworthy African Americans such as Gwendolyn Brooks, Paul Laurence Dunbar, Mary McLeod Bethune, Robert Hayden, and Owen Dodson; and, of course, a poem written in honor of Phillis Wheatley, on the occasion of the bicentennial festival. This ballad, with its easy language and abcb rhyme scheme, reminds the reader of Phillis Wheatley's childhood trip from Africa to the colonies and the terrifying beginning she had in America in simple but powerful language that Walker imagines Phillis speaks:

> *"Boston is a cold town*
> *Ice, and snow, and rain.*
> *Nothing like a tropic world,*
> *nothing like the Plain*
>
> *I have known in Africa:*
> *warm and soft and green.*
> *I am sick for Africa;*
> *take me home again!*
>
> *And I think I cannot bear*
> *all the anguish here:*
> *faces pale and men with whips,*
> *danger always near."*

Margaret Walker herself concludes the poem, carrying the timeline to the present, 1973, and connects Wheatley with her modern-day counterparts at the Phillis Wheatley Poetry Festival, which itself is an "acknowledge[ment of] the power of her work and its continuing impact":

> *Pretty little black girl*
> *no one now can see*
> *all the greatness you will know,*
> *all that you will be.*
>
> *Pretty little black girl*
> *standing on the block*
> *how have you withstood this shame,*
> *bearing all this shock?*

Following the festival, Margaret was a writer in demand. She embarked on a speaking tour in 1974 and received honorary degrees from three different universities: Denison University; her alma mater, Northwestern University; and Rust College. However, even though there were many wonderful recognitions and achievements during the next decade, Margaret also faced legal and medical challenges that would be painful to overcome.

9. Legal Battles

The Cases against Alex Haley and Ellen Wright

Without *Roots*, I never would have known what "fair use" meant.
—*Margaret Walker, from "Conversation: Margaret Walker Alexander and Joanne V. Gabbin"*

*M*argaret's four children were now grown and living their own lives, and in 1975, during the month of October, the month which Margaret had stated earlier held multiple special meanings for her, she received another special gift: her first granddaughter. Joy Dale Alexander was doubly special—not only was she born in October, but she was born on the seventh day of the month, and seven, too, always was an important and lucky number in the life of the new grandmother.

Her happiness was dampened, however, by the publication of a book in 1976 that Margaret believed stole from her now ten-year-old novel, *Jubilee*. Alex Haley's *Roots: The Saga of an American Family* was published on August 17, 1976. Haley's novel was overwhelmingly popular. It won both the Pulitzer Prize and the National Book Award in 1977, and according to *Our Weekly* magazine, it "launched a media blitz, claimed best-seller status and culminated in [a] miniseries that attracted an estimated 130 million viewers. A true cultural phenomenon, it generated a dialogue about race unlike any telecast before or since. Its impact might best be summed up in the following statement from the entry at the Museum of Broadcast Communications website: 'The show defied industry conventions about Black-oriented programming: executives simply had not expected that a show with Black heroes and White villains could attract such huge audiences. In

Margaret Walker at her home surrounded by her grandchildren.
Photograph © Roland L. Freeman.

the process, *Roots* almost single-handedly spawned a new television format—the consecutive-night miniseries."

According to biographer Maryemma Graham, Margaret found "significant parallels between *Jubilee* and Haley's *Roots* . . . to lead her to believe that he had stolen her work." In an interview with Kay Bonetti, Margaret is very explicit about the specific instances of plagiarism:

> I went through *Roots* and found every plagiarized thing. Fifteen scenes from *Jubilee* somehow showed up in *Roots*. . . . There are six characters, most of them with the same names; Chicken George is born on a page in *Jubilee*. There are one hundred and fifty some-odd verbatim expressions. Some part of four hundred pages of *Jubilee* appear in *Roots*.

Margaret sued Haley for copyright infringement, and provided Bonetti with the highlights of the case:

Margaret Walker with Dr. Nick Aaron Ford and Alex Haley (beside plant) before the lawsuit, 1971.

We went to court and the judge said that I was wrong, even though he said in his opening remarks that it was a foregone conclusion that copying had gone on. Then he assigned us to magistrate court. The magistrate sent word back that there was every evidence of plagiarism, that there had been complete access, but she did not have the authority to declare it a case of copyright infringement. The judge must do that. It went back to him and . . . [he] said, "Alex Haley hasn't copied anything from anybody. There are similarities but they're strained, and there's nothing there."

Margaret lost her case, and in bringing the lawsuit brought negative public attention onto herself. However, others sued as well and won. In an article published in January 2013, journalist John Nolte compares Alex Haley to cyclist Lance Armstrong because, he claims, what both men are "most famous for is based on brazen fraud." Even though Margaret was unable to prove her case in court, author Harold Courlander did and won $650,000 in a settlement. Nolte reports that the evidence in the Courlander case was incontrovertible:

> In his Expert Witness Report submitted to federal court, Professor of English Michael Wood of Columbia University stated: "The evidence of copying from [Courlander's book] *The African* in both the novel and the television dramatization of *Roots* is clear and irrefutable. The copying is significant and extensive. . . ."
>
> After a five-week trial in Federal District Court, Courlander and Haley settled the case with a financial settlement and statement that "Alex Haley acknowledges and regrets that various materials from *The African* by Harold Courlander found their way into his book, *Roots*."

Even though she lost the case, Margaret said in an interview with Jacqueline Miller Carmichael that it was time well spent: "I learned all I could find and read about fair use, about copyright infringement.

I learned what it was that the judge had used against me and what case[s] had been against me." It was a valuable lesson as Margaret pursued her next large book project, a profile of a man she had known extremely well: Richard Wright.

The book would not be completed for nine years, and during that time Margaret's writing was interrupted by both joyful and heartbreaking events. Her husband, Alex, was diagnosed with cancer in 1979, the same year Margaret received President Jimmy Carter's "Potentially Unsung Heroes Award." Before his death in 1980, however, Alex would live to see Jackson State honor his wife and her thirty-year teaching career with an all-star retirement tribute and the state of Mississippi proclaim July 12, 1980, "Margaret Walker Alexander Day." Margaret recalls in a 1992 interview with Jacqueline Miller Carmichael that Alex took care of her all her life, and even in his final days he was not thinking about himself but about his wife:

With husband, Alex.

Margaret Walker at her retirement tribute, May 1979. Dr. John A. Peoples, President of Jackson State University, is on her left and Dr. Robert Smith, Dean of Liberal Studies, is on her right.

Margaret Walker Alexander road sign,
Jackson, Mississippi.

Margaret Walker with her mother,
Marion Walker.

Jesse Jackson, 1983.

Before he went to the hospital the last time, he called Siggy and Norma, my son Siggy and [his wife] Norma, sat them down to the table up there and he said, "I want you all to take everything you have in that apartment and come and store it in the back of this house, and I want you to come in here. I don't want to leave Margaret in this house alone when I go to the hospital." Every time those boys went to the hospital, my husband said, "And take care of your mother, and take care of your mother." He told me, he said, "I know you're going to miss me because I would miss you. I want you to know that we've had some wonderful times together. I always wanted my last days to be my best days, and they are; they have been. I want you to continue to be a lady, hold your head high, pay your bills, and try to live." I said that was a sign of his love for me, wasn't it? He was going to look after me when he was gone.

Siggy carried out his father's wishes, and moved into his parents' house with his wife, Norma. Their move was timely, as the name of the street where the house is located received a new moniker: the city of Jackson changed Guynes Street to Margaret Walker Alexander Drive. And in this house on the street named in honor of his mother their first child was born: Sigismund Walker Alexander II.

Although she grieved the loss of her dearly beloved husband, Alex, and her mother, Marion Dozier Walker, three years later, Margaret continued her work on the Richard Wright biography and became increasingly involved with Mississippi politics and the upcoming presidential election. Excited about presidential candidate Jesse Jackson, Margaret served as chairperson of the Mississippi National Rainbow Coalition in 1984, and was elected a delegate to the Democratic National Convention in San Francisco. Margaret describes Jackson in the 1988 essay "Jesse Jackson, the Man, and His Message": "Highly articulate, dynamic and charismatic, [Jackson] has proven himself a national leader with the stature of an international figure." She reveals in that same essay that, as a new delegate, she found the 1984 convention to be a learning experience, and she was physically located too far away from "the center of things" to learn how the political machine worked. In 1988, though, she served as a delegate to the convention again and "lived with the Mississippi delegation and that made the difference." Margaret recalled that Jackson's reception at the 1988 Democratic convention was tremendous; it seemed like "the Jesse Jackson red signs appeared to equal if not outnumber the black signs for [Michael] Dukakis, but that was not the reality. Tuesday was a great day, yet it was an illusion." Dukakis, not Jackson, would win the Democratic nomination:

> When I was asked by news reporters if I would work during the campaign in the fall for Dukakis, I told them I didn't think I would be physically able—too old and sick—and I was sitting in a wheelchair then. Then they inquired, "If it were Jesse Jackson, would you work?" I laughed and said, "Of course, even on crutches."

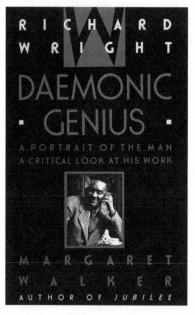

Cover of *Richard Wright, Daemonic Genius.*

Margaret Walker holding a copy of *Daemonic Genius* on her lap.

That same year, 1988, Walker's second big book, *Richard Wright, Daemonic Genius*, was published. Its genesis, however, like *Jubilee*, goes much farther back—in this case to the early 1970s. Horace Cayton, a close friend of Wright's, was working on what Margaret thought would be the authoritative biography of Wright. Cayton, however, died suddenly on January 15, 1970, while doing research in Paris. Margaret tells interviewer Kay Bonetti that "that's the day I knew somebody had to write the book." Although Michael Fabre published a biography of Wright in 1973, Margaret tells Claudia Tate in a 1982 interview that "I felt Wright wanted me to write his biography because nobody [was] going to be more sympathetic and understanding than I."

In the preface to *Richard Wright, Daemonic Genius*, Margaret lays out the "threefold" purpose of her biography:

> [T]o define Richard Wright, to analyze and assess his work, and to show the correlation between the man and his work. I undertook the project because I have been dissatisfied with the work of those who have attempted to do a similar service. Race, creativity, and personal recollection also lead me to make the effort. I believe that Wright is too important to be lost in the confusion of race and politics and racist literary history and criticism so evident in the twentieth century. His personality, literary achievement, and his political significance must be recovered and preserved for posterity.

Margaret proceeded with her biography, even though Wright's widow, Ellen, made publication difficult by refusing to grant Margaret "permission to quote many materials that would further illuminate discussions in this book" unless Margaret allowed her to read the manuscript of the biography first. Margaret refused because, as she writes in the preface to *Daemonic Genius*, "I view[ed] her request as prior restraint tantamount to censorship." Ellen Wright sued Margaret after the unauthorized biography was published, but on September 19, 1990, Margaret had her day in court. The decision in favor of Margaret in *Ellen Wright vs. Warner Books, Inc. and Margaret Walker* was a victory not only for Margaret but, in her opinion, for all writers.

Margaret Walker Alexander Branch Library, Jackson, Mississippi.

The decade of the eighties ended not only with a victory in court, but with more publications and recognitions. In 1988 a branch of the Hinds County Library in Jackson was named in Margaret's honor, and in 1989 the Institute for the Study of History, Life, and Culture of Black People at Jackson State, which she founded in 1968, changed its name to the Margaret Walker Alexander National Research Center for the Study of the Twentieth-Century African American. Margaret also published *This Is My Century: New and Collected Poems*, which included one hundred of her poems, beginning with her prize-winning debut collection *For My People* (along with Stephen Vincent Benét's preface to that volume) as well as the complete collections of *Prophets for a New Day* and *October Journey*. In addition, *This Is My Century* includes thirty new poems and the seven poems Margaret was commissioned by the city of Jackson to write in 1986 in honor of Farish Street, Jackson's historic black district. Additional items of interest in the volume include an illustration of Margaret by artist Elizabeth Catlett, who was Margaret's roommate at Iowa when both were earning their master's degrees. Catlett went on to become a well-known sculptor and printmaker, and this silk screen portrait of Margaret is entitled *For My People—With Love, for Margaret, My*

Friend and was completed in 1987. And the preface Margaret wrote especially for the volume provides an overview of her "life as a poet." As she looks back on the over one thousand poems she has written during her career, she notes that "[a]ll these poems have come out of my living. They express my ideas and emotions about being a woman and a black person in these United States—. . . The South is my home, and my adjustment or accommodation to this South—whether real or imagined (mythic and legendary), violent or nonviolent—is the subject and source of all my poetry. It is also my life."

Margaret Walker and Charlotte Moman, former director of the Margaret Walker Alexander Branch Library. Moman was director of the branch when it was named in Margaret Walker's honor.

Elizabeth Catlett's silk screen portrait of Margaret Walker entitled *For My People—With Love, for Margaret, My Friend.* © Catlett Mora Family Trust/ Licensed by VAGA, New York, New York.

10. Final Years

Awards, Recognitions, and Unfinished Work

She tried to make her life a poem.
—*Margaret Walker's epitaph*

The last ten years of Margaret Walker's life parallels the final decade of the twentieth century, and, perhaps appropriately, the last two published works of Margaret's career during this time are not new works but collections that look back—essays and speeches that reflect and consider both personal memories as well as major themes and ideas of the twentieth century. Her editor, Maryemma Graham, a former student of Walker's who edited both of these volumes—*How I Wrote "Jubilee" and Other Essays on Life and Literature* (1990) and *On Being Female, Black, and Free: Essays by Margaret Walker, 1932–1992* (1997)—says that often the personal and the broader themes Walker addresses are intertwined. In the collection published first, *How I Wrote "Jubilee" and Other Essays on Life and Literature,* Graham describes her challenging job as editor:

> I have compiled what I consider the most representative selections from more than fifty years of a literary life. What I hope I have presented is a vivid, self-told account of the author's life. When I began to make these selections, I did not realize how difficult my task would be. Like the typical editor of essay collections, I posed the "right" questions to myself. Did I want the collection to be mainly autobiographical? Did I want to focus on those essays that were

political, as much of Walker's writing tends to be, or should I favor those essays from which one might deduce Walker's ideas about literary theory and tradition? It did not take me long to realize that such distinctions are not only difficult but almost impossible to make in Walker's case. The activities of Walker's own life, the forces and ideas that have shaped her literary imagination, are inextricably part of and have given shape to the twentieth century as a whole. . . . [V]irtually all of the essays contain elements of autobiography, social history and literary criticism.

The essays provide a wonderful introduction to the life and mind of Margaret Walker, a writer whom Graham feels has not received the critical attention she deserves and "is not included in the standard literary canon" and, as a result, "too few students in today's colleges and universities know her name."

Margaret Walker with Dr. Maryemma Graham at a symposium in the Old Capitol in Jackson, Mississippi, in February 1988. Photograph © David Rae Morris.

Shocking, really, considering the honors and awards she received during the final decade of her life. In 1990 Margaret received the Living Legend Award for Literature from the National Black Arts Festival, and in 1991 she received a Senior Fellowship from the National Endowment for the Humanities for Lifetime Achievement and Contributions to American Literature. In 1992 she was recognized multiple times: by the state of Mississippi with the Governor's Award for Excellence in the Arts; by the College Language Association with the Lifetime Achievement Award; by the AKA Sorority with the Golden Soror Award; and with a tribute along with author Ralph Ellison from the Modern Language Association. She also was honored in a beautiful book of photographs by acclaimed

Margaret Walker with fellow Mississippi writer Eudora Welty at the Governor's Award for Excellence in the Arts, 1992. Governor Kirk Fordice is seated in the background. Photograph by Gil Ford Photography, Inc., courtesy of Charlotte Moman.

Margaret Walker and photographer Roland L. Freeman. Margaret is holding a copy of the book *Margaret Walker's "For My People": A Tribute*, which Freeman published in celebration of the fiftieth anniversary of the publication of her book of poetry *For My People*. They are at the conference "Black Women Writers and Magic Realism" at Jackson State University, 1992. Photograph © Roland L. Freeman.

Margaret Walker, surrounded by graduates, after receiving an honorary degree from Spelman College, Atlanta, Georgia, 1994.

photographer Roland L. Freeman entitled *Margaret Walker's "For My People": A Tribute*, which celebrated the fiftieth anniversary of Walker's award-winning poem and Walker herself. Freeman describes the thirty-eight photographs that he included in an essay that accompanies the images: "I selected photographs that call to mind the special human elements evoked by Walker, so basic to everyday life, and yet not often celebrated, elements which unveil the real beauty and the tenacity for life of African American people." In the midst of all these accolades, Walker, now seventy-seven years old, suffered a minor stroke. Fortunately, her speech and thinking were not affected—only her motor abilities on her left side.

The years 1993–1996 also brought Margaret more awards. In 1993 she received the American Book Award for Lifetime Achievement, and in 1994 she was awarded an honorary degree from Spelman College. In 1995 the Margaret Walker Alexander National Research Center hosted Margaret Walker Alexander Week from November 27 to December 2, and *Ebony* magazine listed Walker as one of the "Fifty Most Important Women in the Past Fifty Years." She also completed the first draft of her autobiography.

In addition to the autobiography, Margaret had other works in various stages of completion. Margaret tells Jerry W. Ward, Jr., in a 1986 interview that she wanted to return to "Goose Island," a novel she wrote during the 1930s that she describes as "flawed," "half-written," and "not very good" and turn it into "a number of short stories" that focus on the characters. She also had four more novels in mind:

> There are four novels left. The sequel to *Jubilee* is one and "Mother Broyer" is another. Th[at] is a novel of the Sixties, Seventies, and Eighties[,] a novel that deals with the period of the Vietnam War, the Civil Rights Movement, the drug scene and the youth subculture. It really deals with the experiences of one of my children. It follows the autobiography [and] Minna and Jim [sequel to *Jubilee*], but it's still [a] family story and Southern-based. And then I've been thinking— I'm not going to rush to do this next one—but, of course, out of the awful experience and fiasco of the litigation surrounding *Jubilee* and *Roots*, there's another novel about this person who wants to get up and over on top without either the integrity or the talent, and what that's like. There's a mighty interesting story there.

Margaret had grand intentions, but the projects she envisioned were never completed. She tells Jacqueline Miller Carmichael that her poor health simply would not allow it: "I got three ideas in my head and I say I'm going to sit to the typewriter, but I haven't been able to type for a year and half. So, you see, I'm handicapped."

Margaret was getting her affairs in order in the 1990s, and one important item she took care of in 1996 was the donation of her personal papers to the Margaret Walker Alexander National Research Center at Jackson State. This generous gift included Walker's literary, administrative, and personal papers and is the centerpiece of the center's manuscript collections. It is, according to the Margaret Walker Alexander National Research Center's website, "One of the single largest collections of a modern, black female writer anywhere in the world." In addition to Margaret's papers, the center "houses more than thirty significant manuscript collections such as the papers of former U.S. Secretary of Education, Roderick Paige, and a large oral history repository that includes the official collection of the Veterans of the Mississippi Civil Rights Movement."

Exterior of Ayer Hall, c. 1904.

The year after Margaret donated her papers to the center, the center moved into its present location, Ayer Hall. The oldest building on the Jackson State campus, Ayer Hall was constructed in 1903. It was named in honor of the first president of the college and was added to the National Register of Historic Places in 1977. It is home to a permanent exhibition that includes artifacts and displays about Walker, as well as temporary exhibits on subjects related to the mission of the center.

In June 1998, at age eighty-two, Margaret Walker was diagnosed with breast cancer. She underwent initial radiation treatment, but decided against surgery. Despite her illness, she still attended several events where she was honored for her lifetime of work. In July 1998, Margaret was recognized along with two other noteworthy Jackson women, author Eudora Welty and International Ballet Competition founder Thalia Mara, at an event celebrating the accomplishments of these "three Grande Dames of Mississippi." She also was inducted into the African American Literary Hall of Fame during the Gwendolyn Brooks Writers' Conference in October, an especially significant honor as she was part of the first class of inductees. The African American Literary Hall of Fame had only just been established at Chicago State University by a group of black publishers and academics "to provide black writers and their philosophies with proper acclaim." The first group of inductees included fourteen living writers—Gwendolyn Brooks, Nikki Giovanni, Toni Morrison,

Eudora Welty (left), Thalia Mara (center), and Margaret Walker, 1998.
Photograph © H. Kay Holloway.

Dudley Randall, and August Wilson, to name a few—and several honored posthumously, such as James Baldwin, W. E. B. Du Bois, Ralph Ellison, Langston Hughes, Zora Neale Hurston, and Richard Wright. Many of the names on this distinguished list reflect both sides of Margaret's life: those who were invaluable teachers to her and those whom she mentored as well.

A month after receiving this distinguished honor, Margaret died from complications of breast cancer at the home of her oldest daughter, Marion, in Chicago. She was eighty-three. Her body lay in state at the Margaret Walker Alexander National Research Center prior to her funeral, which was held in Jackson on December fourth at Central United Methodist Church. Reverend Hickman M. Johnson

Dr. Alferdteen Harrison (second from left), second director of the Margaret Walker Alexander National Research Center, accompanied by Dr. Wanda Macon (in scarf) and an unidentified woman, beside the casket of Margaret Walker, lying in state at the Margaret Walker Alexander National Research Center, Jackson State University, 1998. Photograph © Roland L. Freeman.

presided, and his eulogy was published later in *Farewell, My Friends*, a collection of his most memorable eulogies and tributes. Reverend Johnson celebrates the many hats that Margaret wore:

> Margaret Walker Alexander was a wife, a mother, a friend, a teacher, a scholar, a poet, a writer, a college administrator, a neighbor, and a citizen of the world. She brought honor to this, her adopted state—a state where her family had taught black people for more than a century beginning with her great-uncle, and continuing with her grandfather (a Baptist preacher), her mother, her father (a Methodist preacher), and her sisters. Margaret taught that the "pen [was] mightier than the sword" (Bulwer) and that "words fitly spoken [were] like apples of gold in pictures of silver." (Prov. 25:11)

She was buried beside her beloved husband, Alex, and her epitaph reads simply, "She tried to make her life a poem." To all who knew her and read her works, she succeeded. Her friend Amiri Baraka perhaps said it best in a speech he gave at New York University shortly after her death and which was reprinted in *The Nation*:

Grave marker for Margaret Walker Alexander and her husband, Alex, Garden
Memorial Park, Jackson, Mississippi.

She was one of the greatest writers of the language. She was the
grandest expression of the American poetic voice and the ultimate
paradigm of the Afro-American classic literary tradition. Margaret
Walker Alexander was the living continuum of the great democratic
arts culture that has sustained and inspired the Afro-American people since the middle passage. . . .

From the time she says in her first published work (published by
Du Bois in *The Crisis*), "I want to write," at 19 years old, "I want to
write / I want to write the songs of my people". . . through the great
"For My People" . . . [and] the panoramic drama of her novel *Jubilee*
. . . until her last book of poetry, *This Is My Century* . . . Margaret
stayed on the case. She always stood up. . . . She always spoke with
the open recognizable voice of the people, a tradition she carries as
strongly as Langston Hughes or Sterling Brown.

Baraka is right: from the moment she penned "For My People"
until she completed the poems and preface of *This Is My Century* and
put her pen down due to health issues, Margaret Walker never failed
to find the right words. She found them when she bravely traveled
to Chicago with her younger sister to study at predominantly white

Northwestern University; she found them again when she counted each and every penny in order to travel to the University of Iowa and earn her master's; and she continued to find them as she struggled to make a living, raise a family, and be a wife, mother, and professor of English. Margaret Walker is a testament to perseverance; for thirty years she lived and shaped her great-grandmother's story until she was able to publish it as *Jubilee*, which is not only significant as a best-selling folk novel about slavery but as the manuscript that earned her a long-sought-after Ph.D. Perhaps she did not even recognize her own achievements: breaking the color barrier when she became a member of the Poetry Society of America at Northwestern; or breaking both the color and gender barriers when she was the first black woman to attend Yaddo; or establishing one of the first black studies departments in the country. Hers was a voice for both the past and present, as Baraka so eloquently pays tribute:

Margaret Walker remains part of our deepest and most glorious voice, dimensioned by history and musicked by vision. . . . That voice to keep us live and sane and strong and ready to fight and even ready to love. Like our mothers' mothers' mothers' mothers' mothers' mother and our wives and sisters and our daughters and our comrades and our mothers' mothers' mothers' mothers' mother, Margaret Walker Alexander.

Afterword

The Legacy of Margaret Walker

In a 1992 interview with Jacqueline Miller Carmichael, Margaret Walker was very clear that she wanted her papers to be stored in a center at Jackson State University bearing her name. Even when the opportunity arose for her papers to go to the Library of Congress, she was insistent that they stay at her university for all to have access to them: "And when I'm told that my papers should go to the Library of Congress, I remind them that all the Library of Congress will do with my papers is take them to the basement where they have all the Indian artifacts. They're not going to process them and microfilm them and set them up for scholarly research. That's what I want done with my papers."

And when the Amistad Center at Tulane University offered her papers a home, she declined because of unhappy memories of segregation during her time in New Orleans: "When I was seventeen . . . I could not walk across the campus of Tulane. There was a man there who read my poetry, but Jewish friends had to take it. I couldn't take it to him. And I would feel very bad now, remembering segregation and Tulane, to give them my papers. The white universities don't need my papers; the black students in the black colleges are the ones who need my papers."

Margaret Walker got her wish: the Institute for the Study of the History, Life, and Culture of Black People, which she founded in 1968 at Jackson State (and was renamed the Margaret Walker Alexander National Research Center in 1989) became the repository of all her papers in 1996.

Margaret would be amazed at the growth of her center since her death in 1998. After Margaret retired from Jackson State, the second

Margaret Walker and Dr. Alferdteen Harrison discussing programs for the Margaret
Walker Alexander National Research Center. They are in Margaret's home, Jackson,
Mississippi, 1992. Photograph © Roland L. Freeman.

director of the center, Dr. Alferdteen Harrison, took the institute to
the next level. A professor of history at Jackson State for many years,
she increased the holdings of the center, especially in the areas of oral
history and preservation. She dramatically increased the oral history
collection, "adding interviews to the general oral history collection for
twenty years, from 1974 to 1994 . . . The goal was to document almost
all facets of African-American life and history. Among the topics
covered are integration, black churches, the civil rights movement,
rural life, women's issues, black businesses, and the history of Jackson
State University." In addition, she oversaw the renovation and move
of the center into historic Ayer Hall, the oldest building on Jackson
State's campus, making it suitable as an archive and storage facility.

Margaret never saw her center move into its current home. It's a
beautiful building—sitting on the main campus behind a grove of
oaks—the only building at Jackson State that resembles a house,
and it welcomes visitors with its steep step entrance and lovely front
porch. A permanent exhibit devoted to the life of Margaret Walker is
maintained on one side of the first floor; on the other is the Roderick
Paige Reading Room where scholars can request archival materials.

Exterior of Ayer Hall, home to the Margaret Walker Alexander National Research Center.

The building is four levels, and the other floors house offices and storage facilities. There also are additional rooms which showcase temporary exhibitions.

Dr. Harrison retired in 2007. Angela Stewart, archivist at the center, was named interim head and served for two years until Dr. Robert Luckett was hired in 2009. Dr. Luckett is continuing the work of both Dr. Walker and Dr. Harrison, and is expanding the center even further. This is, perhaps, the most exciting chapter in the life of the center, as a brand-new building has been designed to meet the center's needs. According to a feasibility study that Dr. Luckett authored, serious environmental problems exist within Ayer Hall that need to be addressed if it is to continue to serve as an archive:

> The manuscript vaults on the first floor and the oral history vault on the third floor are nearing their capacities and have significant environmental issues. While limited space to grow the Center's collections is a problem, the building's issues with temperature and humidity control are not sustainable for an archive. Not only that, exposed

water piping runs along the ceiling of the Center's manuscript vaults and is a grave concern, but even more problematic is the water moisture issue. The first three floors of Ayer Hall were never properly insulated so that water seeps through the walls on rainy days and has led to mildew and mold. These problems merit serious consideration, but, due to the fact that Ayer Hall has been on the National Register of Historic Places since 1977, there are constraints on what can be done to fix these problems.

In order to address these issues as well as look towards the future, Dr. Luckett has teamed up with the university architect and designed a state-of-the-art facility that not only resolves the immediate problem of adequate storage space and optimum conditions for archival materials, but expands the Margaret Walker Center into a true museum, archives, and learning center. After spending much of the last two years visiting black cultural centers and museums all over the country, Dr. Luckett, Angela Stewart, and Jackson State graduate students in art and urban and regional planning took the best of what they saw and gathered, and went to work with the Jackson State architect to design a building that would be true to Margaret's vision and fit in with expansion plans for the entire university.

Margaret Walker Alexander National Research Center today.

Margaret Walker exhibit inside the Margaret Walker Alexander National Research Center. Her desk, typewriter, photograph of her children, bust of Margaret Walker by sculptor Harold S. Dorsey, copies of *Jubilee* and *On Being Female, Black and Free: Essays by Margaret Walker, 1932–1992*, and a favorite hat are on display.

Gift Shop of the Margaret Walker Alexander National Research Center.

The design for the proposed building centers around Margaret Walker's own hands. Why hands? Marlin King, the architect, explains:

[W]e chose to use the hands of Dr. Margaret Walker Alexander as a tribute to black women as a whole. Over the centuries, these beautiful hands have produced great works of literature, song, dance, art, stage, and film. They have nurtured generations, endured shackles, raised families, fed the hungry, cared for the sick, been raised in defiance of unjust laws, educated students, picked cotton, woven baskets, and offered wise counsel. . . .

Hands are the main structures for manipulating the environment, much in the way that architecture alters the landscape or the Margaret Walker Center can change the lives of its patrons. As light is only able to transmit through the four spaces between the fingers of the hand, so it is with this proposed building: four prominent areas that receive and/or give light.

The four light spaces of the new center include floor-to-ceiling glass walls enclosing studios for visiting artists; a 150-seat auditorium and changing exhibition space which allows natural diffused light into the gallery; a reading room that "features a visual interpretation of Walker's poem "For My People" and serves "as a screen tint allowing natural light into the reading room"; and nontraditional classrooms overlooking a courtyard "to stimulate learning in various environments."

Perhaps most exciting of all is the new exhibit devoted to Walker herself. In Ayer Hall, the permanent exhibit about Walker's life covers approximately 250 square feet; in the new center the exhibit will be expanded to 1,300 square feet and will not only cover her life but also offer an in-depth exploration of the novel *Jubilee*, a "'Writer's Connection' gallery that examines the links between Walker and other writers of the 20th Century, and a gallery to engage the young children who visit the Margaret Walker Center."

Dr. Luckett hopes to see construction of the new Margaret Walker Center during the year of Walker's centennial: 2015. Even when the future center is finally built and Margaret Walker's papers find a beautiful, new, environmentally sound home, the Margaret Walker

Alexander National Research Center will have already accomplished what Margaret Walker originally envisioned: a place for learning and a public recognition of the importance of the black voice in the study of literature and culture.

Acknowledgments

---

*F*irst and foremost, I would like to thank the Margaret Walker Center: Director Dr. Robert Luckett, Archivist Angela Stewart, and the entire staff at the Center at Jackson State University for their generous support of my book. From retrieving materials from the archives, supplying photographs, granting interviews, and connecting me with individuals who could assist me with my research to allowing me to take photographs on the premises, they gave invaluable assistance. I absolutely could not have written this book without them. It was always wonderful to be greeted with a smile and a hug—thank you, Robby, Angela, and Trina.

I also want to thank two individuals who have inspired me with their own publications on the life of Margaret Walker and who have paved the way for others like myself: Dr. Maryemma Graham and Dr. William R. Ferris. Dr. Graham made time to have coffee with me on one of her quick trips to Jackson and was enthusiastic about my book. She has answered many, many questions via e-mail, and I appreciate her generosity of time and support as I know she is working on her own biography of Walker. All who do research on Margaret Walker owe Dr. Graham a huge debt of gratitude for her outstanding scholarship and research on the life and works of Margaret Walker.

And Dr. William R. Ferris, Senior Associate Director of the Center for the Study of the American South at UNC–Chapel Hill, was as generous and kind regarding this biography as he was with my first. Thank you, Bill, for sending me wonderful photographs of Margaret Walker before I had to ask!

I also would like to thank the following individuals and institutions for their support and contributions to *Song of My Life*:

photographer Roland L. Freeman; photographer David Rae Morris; photographer Roy Lewis; Linden Anderson, Jr., with the Schomburg Center for Research in Black Culture at the New York Public Library; Cynthia Fife-Townsel, Harsh Collection, Chicago Public Library; Karen Spicher, Beinecke Rare Book and Manuscript Library, Yale University; Morgan Jones, Wilson Special Collections Library, UNC–Chapel Hill; Don Veasey, Department of Archives and Manuscripts, Birmingham Public Library; Michael Campbell, Archives, Dillard University; Janet C. Olson, University Archives, Northwestern University; Jeffrey Bruce, Director of Exhibitions and Collections, Tubman African American Museum, Macon, Georgia; Randy Klein, composer of *For My People: The Margaret Walker Song Cycle*; and Dr. Alferdteen Harrison, Dr. Jerry W. Ward, Jr., and Charlotte Moman at the Eudora Welty Library in Jackson, Mississippi, who provided photographs, invaluable information, and support. I look forward to working with the three of them, the staff of the Welty Library, and all involved on events planned for Margaret Walker's centennial in 2015.

In addition, I would like to thank the following agencies and institutions for permission to quote or use materials in their possession: the Margaret Walker Alexander National Research Center, University Press of Mississippi, the University of Georgia Press, the University of Tennessee Press, the Feminist Press, Harper Collins, *The Nation*, the estate of Elizabeth Catlett, and the Limited Editions Club.

I also owe a debt of gratitude to my friend Sarah Campbell, my writing partner/photographer, who is always a source of useful and important information on writing, publishing, children's literature, photography, and sending sons off to college! She also introduced me to Roderick Red of Red Squared Productions, who spent the day with Sarah and me taking photographs at the Margaret Walker Center and Jackson State. Thank you, Roderick. And thanks, too, to Sarah's mother, Patty Crosby, who shared the wonderful photograph of Margaret Walker speaking at Port Gibson High School's commencement when Sarah's older sister, Emilye, gave the valedictory address.

Another friend who went above and beyond is Carla Wall, to whom I dedicate *Song of My Life*. Not only did she participate in road trips and research; she also unearthed invaluable documents and photographs. And she was a fantastic driver around areas of Jackson and New Orleans with which I was unfamiliar. I can't thank you enough, Carla.

Finally, thanks to my two families: first, my University Press of Mississippi family—Leila, John, Valerie, Anne, Carol, Steve, Shane, and Clint—who birthed my first book, enthusiastically supported my second, and are primed to do a third! You all know the important roles you play in the magic of creating and bringing out both of my books. Thank you. And thanks to my wonderfully supportive family: my parents, Jon and Sandra Kates; brothers, Michael and David; husband, Lus, and my two sons, Will and Sam. I love you all very much.

Appendix 1

Chronology of Margaret Walker's Life

I wish to acknowledge my debt to Dr. Maryemma Graham, who wrote the first chronology of Margaret Walker's life, which can be found in *Fields Watered with Blood: Critical Essays on Margaret Walker* (Athens: University of Georgia Press, 2001), xix–xxvii.

1915 Born July 7 in Birmingham, Alabama, to Reverend Sigismund Constantine Walker and Marion Dozier Walker; grandmother Elvira Ware Dozier moves in with family

1920 Family moves to Meridian, Mississippi; Walker begins school

1925 Family moves to New Orleans, Louisiana

1930 Graduates from Gilbert Academy (age fourteen); enters New Orleans University (present-day Dillard University) for college

1931 Wins College Freshman Writing Prize

1932 Publishes first essay, "What Is to Become of Us?" in *Our Youth*, a New Orleans magazine; meets Langston Hughes; enrolls in Northwestern University in Chicago as a junior

1934 Meets W. E. B. Du Bois in Chicago; he publishes her first poem, "Daydream," in *Crisis*

1935 Begins novel *Jubilee*; graduates from Northwestern University with a B.A. in English (age twenty)

1936 Joins Federal Writers' Project as junior writer; meets Richard Wright and joins the South Side Writers' Group

1937 Publishes "For My People" in *Poetry* in November issue

1938 Publishes poems in *Poetry*, *Opportunity*, and *New Challenge*

1939 Enters University of Iowa for graduate school

1940 Graduates from University of Iowa with M.A.

1941 Publishes "For My People" in *Negro Caravan*

1942 Joins faculty of Livingstone College, Salisbury, North Carolina, for spring semester; joins English Department at West Virginia State College for fall semester; wins Yale Series of Younger Poets award; *For My People* published; meets Firnist James Alexander

1943 Marries Firnist James "Alex" Alexander on June 13 in High Point, North Carolina; attends first black college professional conference (College Language Association); attends Yaddo; signs with the National Artists and Concert Corporation

1944 First child and daughter, Marion Elizabeth, born; receives Rosenwald Fellowship which allows her to do research on *Jubilee*; Elvira Ware Dozier dies

1945 Returns to Livingstone College to teach

1946 Second child and first son, Firnist James Alexander, Jr., born

1949 Third child, Sigismund Constantine, born; joins English Department of Jackson State College, Jackson, Mississippi

1952 Organizes 75th Jubilee Anniversary of Jackson State College (October 19–24)

1953 Father dies; receives Ford Fellowship which allows her to do research on *Jubilee*

1954 Fourth child, Margaret Elvira, born

1955 Moves to house on Guynes Street (in 1957 becomes the neighbor of Medgar and Myrlie Evers)

1961 Returns to University of Iowa and enters doctoral program

1962 Begins two-year leave from Jackson State to work on Ph.D.

1965 Earns Ph.D. from University of Iowa

1966 *Jubilee* published

1968 Establishes the Institute for the Study of the History, Life, and Culture of Black People at Jackson State

1973 Hosts Phillis Wheatley (bicentennial) Poetry Festival at Jackson State

1977 Files suit against Alex Haley, author of *Roots*, for plagiarism

1978 Jackson State University sponsors "Margaret Walker: A Woman for All Seasons" retirement tribute

1980   July 12 proclaimed "Margaret Walker Alexander Day" by Mississippi Governor William Winter; husband, Alex, dies (November)

1981   Guynes Street renamed Margaret Walker Alexander Drive

1983   Mother dies

1984   Elected delegate to Democratic National Convention and serves as chairperson, Mississippi National Rainbow Coalition supporting Jesse Jackson for President

1988   Branch of Hinds County library renamed Margaret Walker Alexander Library

1989   The Institute for the Study of the History, Life, and Culture of Black People at Jackson State renamed the Margaret Walker Alexander National Research Center for the Study of the Twentieth-Century African American

1991   Receives senior fellowship from the National Endowment for the Humanities for Lifetime Achievement and Contributions to American Literature

1992   Hospitalized for minor stroke; attends "Black Women Writers and Magic Realism" conference at Jackson State, which commemorated the fiftieth anniversary of the publication of *For My People*

1995   The Margaret Walker Alexander National Research Center for the Study of the Twentieth-Century African American hosts "Margaret Walker Alexander Week" (November 27– December 2)

1996   Donates private papers to the Margaret Walker Alexander National Research Center

1998   Diagnosed with cancer (June), dies in Chicago on November 30, funeral in Jackson on December 4

Appendix 2

List of Major Published Works

To find Margaret Walker's poems in anthologies, a list of selected criticism, reviews, and translations, see the "Selected Bibliography of Works by and about Margaret Walker," created by Bernice Bell and Robert Harris in *Fields Watered with Blood: Critical Essays on Margaret Walker* (Athens: University of Georgia Press, 2001), 321–40.

1932   "What Is to Become of Us?," *Our Youth*

1934   "Daydream," *Crisis*

1937   "For My People," *Poetry*

1941   "For My People," *Negro Caravan*

1942   *For My People*, Yale University Press

1943   "Growing Out of Shadow," *Common Ground*

1951   "How I Told My Child About Race," *Negro Digest*

1966   *Jubilee*, Houghton Mifflin

1970   *Prophets for a New Day*, Broadside Press

1972   *How I Wrote "Jubilee,"* Third World Press

1973   *October Journey*, Broadside Press

1974   *A Poetic Equation: Conversations between Nikki Giovanni and Margaret Walker*, Howard University Press

1975   "Chief Worshipers at All World Altars," *Encore*

1976   "Some Aspects of the Black Aesthetic," *Freedomways*

1986   *For Farish Street*, Jackson Arts Alliance

1988   *Richard Wright, Daemonic Genius*, Amistad Press

1989   *This Is My Century: New and Collected Poems*, University of Georgia Press

1990   *How I Wrote "Jubilee" and Other Essays on Life and Literature*, ed. Maryemma Graham, Feminist Press

Margaret Walker, seated beside Charlotte Moman, former director of the Margaret Walker Alexander Library, celebrating the publication of *On Being Female, Black, and Free: Essays by Margaret Walker, 1932–1992*, at the Margaret Walker Alexander Library, Jackson, Mississippi, 1997.

1997   *On Being Female, Black, and Free: Essays by Margaret Walker, 1932–1992*, ed. Maryemma Graham, University of Tennessee Press

2013   *This Is My Century: New and Collected Poems*, reissued by University of Georgia Press

Appendix 3

Major Honors and Awards

1931 College Freshman Writing Prize, New Orleans University

1942 Yale Series of Younger Poets Award for *For My People*

1944 Receives Rosenwald Fellowship

1953 Receives Ford Fellowship

1966 Houghton Mifflin Literary Award

1966 Mable Carney Student National Education Association Plaque for Scholar-Teacher of the Year

1966 Alpha Kappa Alpha Sorority Citation for Advancement of Knowledge

1968 Receives key to city from New Orleans Mayor Victor Schiro

1972 Receives National Endowment for the Humanities Senior Fellowship

1974 Receives Doctor of Literature from Northwestern University

1974 Receives Doctor of Literature from Rust College

1974 Receives Doctor of Fine Arts from Denison University

1979 Awarded emerita status by Jackson State University

1979 Receives "Potentially Unsung Heroes Award" from President Jimmy Carter

1980 July 12 declared "Margaret Walker Alexander Day" by Mississippi Governor William Winter

1982 Receives W. E. B. Du Bois Award from Association of Social and Behavioral Scientists

1990 Receives Living Legend Award for Literature from National Black Arts Festival

1991 Receives Senior Fellowship from the National Endowment for the Humanities for Lifetime Achievement and Contributions to American Literature

Margaret Walker receiving an honorary degree from Spelman College, 1994. Spelman
President Johnnetta B. Cole is pictured on the right.

1992   Receives Lifetime Achievement Award from the College
        Language Association
1992   Receives Governor's Award for Excellence in the Arts
        (Mississippi)
1992   Receives Golden Soror Award from Alpha Kappa Alpha
        Sorority
1992   Receives tribute, with Ralph Ellison, from the Modern
        Language Association
1993   Receives American Book Award for Lifetime Achievement
1994   Receives Honorary Degree from Spelman College
1995   Named by *Ebony* magazine as one of "Fifty Most Important
        Women in the Past Fifty Years"
1996   Receives John Hurt Fisher Award from South Atlantic
        Association of Departments of English
1998   Receives Arts Achievement Award, Jackson, Mississippi
1998   Inducted into the African American Literary Hall of Fame

Appendix 4

Major Adaptations, Recordings, Editions, Dramatic Performances, and Artwork Inspired by Margaret Walker's Work

❦

1975 *Margaret Walker Reads Margaret Walker and Langston Hughes; Poetry of Margaret Walker Read by Margaret Walker;* and *Margaret Walker Reads Langston Hughes, Paul Laurence Dunbar, and James Weldon,* all recorded by Smithsonian Folkways Recordings

1976 Premiere of Ulysses Kay's adaptation of *Jubilee* by OperaSouth

Reception following the opening of the opera *Jubilee,* based on Margaret Walker's novel, Jackson, Mississippi, 1976. Photograph © Roland L. Freeman.

Margaret Walker, center, surrounded by her family, at the reception following the opening of the opera *Jubilee*, Jackson, Mississippi, 1976. Photograph © Roland L. Freeman.

1984   Daughters of Margaret Walker Alexander, a professional arts ensemble which performs the poetry of Margaret Walker, founded in Jackson, Mississippi

From the press release:

Dr. Rosia Wade Crisler is the director of the troupe, which is made up of Vergia Dishman (soloist), Bridget Archer (dancer), and Charles Dillon (pianist). . . . The group has been performing for many community organizations and touring college and university circuits since 1987 . . . The ensemble artistically fuses dramatizations of the writings of Margaret Walker Alexander and other African American writers with music. All performances emphasize the positive attributes and contributions of African Americans and women to promote race and gender pride.

Page from the limited edition of *For My People* which contains five multicolored lithographs by artist Elizabeth Catlett. This image accompanies the stanza: "For my playmates in the clay and dust and sand of Alabama backyards playing baptizing and preaching and doctor and jail and soldier and school and mama and cooking and playhouse and concert and store and hair and Miss Choomby and company." © Catlett Mora Family Trust/Licensed by VAGA, New York, New York.

1992 *For My People*, five multicolored lithographs created by artist Elizabeth Catlett in an oversize volume (18½" x 22½") for the Limited Editions Club. There are only four hundred numbered copies, each signed by both Margaret Walker and Elizabeth Catlett.

From the publisher:

Each of the poem's ten stanzas was hand set in thirty point Albertus type, a sans serif face that looks as if chiseled from granite and printed letterpress on French made Arches cover paper, the same paper upon which were printed the Elizabeth Catlett lithographs. The book is bound in imported red Japanese linen over heavy boards, the box is covered in black cotton. Each book is signed by Margaret Walker and Elizabeth Catlett. 1992. Value: $1,500.

Margaret Walker, center, reading poetry in the den of her home, surrounded by family and friends, in Jackson, Mississippi, 1992. Photographer Roland L. Freeman took this photograph, and it is included in his book of photographs *Margaret Walker's "For My People": A Tribute*, University Press of Mississippi, 1992. Photograph © Roland L. Freeman.

1992 *Margaret Walker's "For My People": A Tribute*, Roland Freeman, University Press of Mississippi

From the photographer:

This photo essay is my tribute to the rich cultural depths of Margaret Walker's classic poetry collection, *For My People*, and explores the impact of her poetry upon me. Each of the photographs seeks to capture the spirit of the people about whom Margaret Walker sings. . . .

Walker's lines are illuminating, provocative, and reverential, and I have tried to select photographs with those same qualities, regardless of their specific content relationship to any of the individual poems. In all the photographs, Walker's imagery and narratives have been interpreted through the photographic odyssey of my career.

2009 *Lineage: A Margaret Walker Song Cycle*, musical performance/adaptation of Margaret Walker's *For My People* by composer Randy Klein, Kansas University Hall Center for the Humanities, Lawrence, Kansas

2012 *For My People: The Margaret Walker Song Cycle*, multimedia performance featuring composer Randy Klein, vocalist Aurelia Williams, and members of the Jackson State Chorale, Jackson, Mississippi

A performance of *For My People: The Margaret Walker Song Cycle*—a new musical work by composer Randy Klein based on the poems of Margaret Walker—at San Diego State University School of Music and Dance, March 24, 2013. The concert featured composer Randy Klein on piano, vocal solos by Broadway performer Aurelia Williams, the eighty-voice Aztec Concert Choir under the direction of Dr. Patrick Walders, and choral arrangements by James Ballard.

For My People by artist Cedric Colston, 2012. Acrylic on canvas. It hangs in the Margaret Walker exhibit area of the Margaret Walker Alexander National Research Center.

From the press release:

The Song Cycle is a musical work that incorporates the poetry of Margaret Walker and the music of Randy Klein. It is an exciting multi-media performance that combines a musical concert with video projections corresponding to the images in the poetry and rare footage of Walker reading her poetry. These art songs paint musical impressions to match the poet's intentions. . . .

2012 *For My People* by artist Cedric Colston; acrylic on canvas

From the artist's notes:

This piece was inspired by the late Margaret Walker Alexander. It is a painting of a photograph of her taken by Carl Van Vechten. The words in the background are from her famous poem "For My People." The legacy that she left behind is a great inspiration and a positive example to follow.

2015 *For My People: The Margaret Walker Song Cycle*, to be performed in various venues in Mississippi during Margaret Walker's centennial year

From an interview:

Composer Randy Klein is adding new pieces to *For My People: The Margaret Walker Song Cycle*, which has grown substantially since it debuted in 2009.

Neighborhood Garden Club (Guynes Street). Myrlie Evers, widow of Medgar Evers, stands in the center behind the punch bowl; Margaret Walker is second from right.

Margaret Walker with fellow Mississippi writers. Seated front Ellen Douglas (left) and Betty Werlein Carter (center); in back Shelby Foote (left) and Bern Keating.

Margaret Walker giving the commencement address at Port Gibson High School, 1983.

Margaret Walker, photographed by Carl Van Vechten, 1942.

Margaret Walker with her husband Firnist James Alexander.

Margaret Walker is at the Beinecke Rare Book and Manuscript Library, Yale University, New Haven, Connecticut, 1978. She was researching her correspondence with Richard Wright for her forthcoming book *Richard Wright, Daemonic Genius*.

In this picture, Margaret Walker Alexander is surrounded by four distinguished professors of southern literature: from left to right, Lewis Simpson from Louisiana State University and editor of *The Southern Review*; Dan Young from Vanderbilt; Blyden Jackson from Southern University in Baton Rouge and later the University of North Carolina–Chapel Hill; and Louis Rubin, also from UNC–Chapel Hill. This picture was taken on the front porch of Rowan Oak, home of William Faulkner, Oxford, Mississippi.

Margaret Walker with Dr. Jerry W. Ward, Jr., at the "Black Women Writers and Magic Realism" conference, Jackson State University, October 1992. Photograph © Roland L. Freeman.

Margaret Walker at Square Books in Oxford, Mississippi, in 1988 at a signing of her book *Richard Wright, Daemonic Genius.*

Margaret Walker at the Margaret Walker Alexander National Research Center, Jackson State University, 1988. Photograph © Roland L. Freeman.

Abbreviations Used in the Notes

AAR	African American Registry
ARC	Amistad Research Center
BAC	Biography from Answers.com
BAP	*Black American Poets Between Worlds, 1940–1960*
BB	Brietbart.com
BWW	*Black Women Writers at Work*
CP	"Composer and Pianist Randy Klein"
DG	*Richard Wright, Daemonic Genius*
DMW	Daughters of Margaret Walker Alexander
DSU	Delta State University
EOC	*Encyclopedia of Chicago*
FBF	*On Being Female, Black and Free: Essays by Margaret Walker, 1932–1992*
FF	*The Furious Flowering of African American Poetry*
FMF	*Farewell, My Friends!*
FMP	*For My People*
FWB	*Fields Watered with Blood: Critical Essays on Margaret Walker*
HWJ	*How I Wrote "Jubilee" and Other Essays on Life and Literature*
ITT	*In These Times*
JSU	Jackson State University
LEC	The Limited Editions Club
MDA	Mississippi Development Authority
MET	Mississippi Educational Television
MQ	*Mississippi Quarterly*
MR	*Missouri Review*

MWAT   *Margaret Walker's "For My People": A Tribute*
MWC   Margaret Walker Center
MWFS   Margaret Walker Center Feasibility Study
MWT   *Mississippi Writers Talking*
NGE   *"Jubilee," The New Georgia Encyclopedia*
OHP   *The Black Women Oral History Project at the Schlesinger Library, Radcliffe College*
OW   *Our Weekly*
PF   "Margaret Walker 1915–1998," The Poetry Foundation
PND   *Prophets for a New Day*
PW   *Publishers Weekly*
SL   *Southern Living* magazine
TFS   *Trumpeting a Fiery Sound: History and Folklore in Margaret Walker's "Jubilee"*
TMC   *This Is My Century: New and Collected Poems*
TN   *The Nation*
UA   Unpublished Autobiography

Source Notes

Full citations for the sources can be found in the bibliography.

EPIGRAPH

Page
vii   "I wonder if I": "A Writer for Her People: An Interview with Dr. Margaret Walker
       Alexander," MQ, p. 522.

AUTHOR'S NOTE

xi   "the most famous": "Introduction," FWB, p. 1.
xi   "Mississippi's Literary Trail": SL, p. 1.
xi   "the Margaret Walker Center,": SL, p. 1.

CHAPTER ONE
Childhood: Creativity on Display

3   "It seems as if": UA, p. 41.
3   "my first acquaintance": UA, p. 54.
3   "nature, race, and religion": UA, p. 49.
3   "During my adolescence": UA, p. 3.
4   "was inclined to": UA, p. 55.
4   "conceive of a hundred": UA, p. 55.
4   "I have never seen": UA, p. 55.
4   "At home and school": UA, p. 55.
4   "I have never forgotten": UA, p. 55.
5   "lifetime favorites": UA, p. 56.
5   "The first time": UA, p. 56.
6   "had no great admiration": "Margaret Walker Alexander," MWT, p. 127.

7   "On the way": "Margaret Walker Alexander," MWT, p. 122.

7   "Both my parents": UA, p. 14.

8   "happy year . . .": UA, p. 25.

8   "Mama says" and "Mama says": UA, p. 28.

9   "a real achievement": UA, p. 29.

9   "with two large": UA, p. 29.

10   "which soon bore": UA, p. 29.

10   "a long way," "three little white" and "she don't know": UA, p. 36.

10   "Daddy was so happy": UA, pp. 30–31.

10   "As a very young child": "Interview with Margaret Walker," MET, 4 August 1983.

11   "Mama was always": UA, pp. 43–44.

11   "That fire was": UA, pp. 33–34.

12   "[t]he end of": UA, p. 45.

CHAPTER TWO
Education: New Orleans and Chicago

13   "I am sure": UA, p. 57.

13   "great excitement of": UA, p. 48.

13   "Latin—Caesar": UA, p. 48.

13   "the American Negro's": UA, p. 50.

15   "If you will": UA, p. 50.

15   "she said we were": UA, p. 52.

16   "My teacher": UA, p. 53.

17   "Are you thinking" and "shook": UA, p. 54.

17   "that if they": UA, p. 54.

17   "all the music": UA, p. 57.

18   "losing interest": UA, p. 57.

18   "were all dust": UA, p. 58.

18   "[w]e carried food": UA, p. 58.

19   "Of course there": UA, p. 58.

19   "broiling hot": UA, p. 58.

19   "straight up the": UA, p. 59.

19   "They don't dance": UA, p. 59.

19   "[F]or the first": UA, p. 59.

21   "I shall remember": UA, p. 60.

21   "[t]hose first few": UA, p. 91.

22   "forty Negroes": UA, p. 6.

22   "teachers told darky": UA, p. 6.

22   "were at the mercy": UA, p. 6.

22   "meat, chicken, pies": UA, p. 91.

22   "take several sophomore": UA, p. 91.

22   "which I was very grateful" and "nearly killed me": UA, p. 92.

22   "Aristotle's *Poetics*, Plato's": UA, p. 91.

22   "devoured them" and "[t]his began a": UA, pp. 91–92.

22   "Under Hungerford": "I Want to Write," FWB, p. 16.

23   "When she turned in": "I Want to Write," FWB, p. 16.

23   "[a]pparently, Hungerford": "I Want to Write," FWB, p. 27.

23   "I went up to": UA, pp. 83–84.

24   "I want to write": "I Want to Write," FWB, p. 17.

CHAPTER THREE

Chicago: Richard Wright and the South Side Writers' Group

25   "Chicago was a": UA, p. 80.

25   "Italy was moving": UA, p. 82.

25   "We went to work": UA, p. 96.

26   "a few dollars": UA, p. 89.

26   "You don't remember": UA, p. 96.

27   "[W]e were on": UA, p. 90.

27   "radical white women": "I Want to Write," FWB, p. 21.

27   "in which the Communist": DG, p. 70.

27   "In Chicago": "I Want to Write," FWB, p. 20.

28   "Over 800 delegates": EOC, p. 1.

28   "I tried to": DG, p. 71.

28   "Twice I left": DG, pp. 71–72.

29   "I asked [Wright]": UA, pp. 85–86.

29   "was surprised to": DG, p. 72.

29–30 "were kind in their" and "... Wright was the": DG, p. 72.

30   "I spent most": DG, p. 72.

30   "... I recognized at once": UA, p. 86.

31   "One afternoon as": DG, pp. 74–75.

31   "We sat together": DG, p. 76.

32   "Negro spirituals": DG, 76.

32   "moves closer to": "I Want to Write," FWB, p. 23.

32   "I want my body": "I Want to Write," FWB, p. 23.

CHAPTER FOUR

Chicago: Life After Northwestern

33   "Thus ended my": UA, p. 104.

33   "I was considered": UA, p. 90.

33   "reading poetry and": UA, p. 91.

33   "Listen, Margaret": UA, p. 91.

34   "Southern trees bear": UA, p. 91.

34   "It was the": UA, p. 92.

34   "Mercedes was shocked": UA, p. 91.

35   "rarely did he": UA, p. 92.

35   "We couldn't manage": UA, p. 93.

36   "I remember Wright": "Margaret Walker," BWW, p. 195.

36   "social conditions": "A Writer for Her People: An Interview with Dr. Margaret
Walker Alexander," MQ, p. 522.

37   "It was Saturday morning": UA, p. 97.

37   "Young, naive, green": UA, p. 100.

37   "but I was so": UA, p. 98.

37   "sophisticated lad[ies]": UA, p. 99.

37   "showed me the sights": UA, p. 99.

38   "[i]t was a": UA, p. 100.

38   "I knew I must": UA, p. 100.

38   "a gathering place": "Vivian Gordon Harsh," BAC, p. 2.

38   "There was a big": UA, pp. 100–101.

38   "if my work": UA, p. 101.

39   "When I received": UA, p. 104.

39   "I was not in": UA, p. 104.

CHAPTER FIVE

Iowa: Writing "For My People"

40   "Twice I have gone": UA, p. 109.

40   "stared at me," "You're Margaret" and "Yes, Sir": UA, p. 110.

40   "a new experiment": UA, p. 110.

41   "A creative person": UA, p. 110.

41   "they had to search": UA, p. 111.

41   "[I] owed nobody": UA, p. 112.

41   "remarkable teachers" and "Austin Warren": UA, p. 99.

42   "constantly clash[ing]," "I thought he," and "were [all] in": UA, p. 100.

42   "Negro ballads": UA, p. 101.

42   "the bottom dropped": UA, p. 103.

43   "I passed [my exams]": UA, p. 108.

43   "Dear Miss Walker": UA, p. 108.

43   "I sent thirty-five": UA, p. 127.

44   "almost entirely by": UA, p. 128.

44   "In a matter of days": UA, p. 129.

45   "That year, 1942": "Margaret Walker," BWW, p. 192.

45   "before somebody else": UA, 7.

45   "The night I": "Black Women in Academia," HWJ, p. 29.

46   "When I knocked": UA, p. 8.

47   ". . . in whatever": "Foreword," FMP, p. 8.

47   "illustrious start" and "Winning the Yale": "Looking Back: A Conversation with Margaret Walker," MWAT, p. 11.

47   "[i]n 1942, when": "Margaret Walker: Folk Orature and Historical Prophecy," BAP, p. 106.

CHAPTER SIX

Writing *Jubilee*: A Balancing Act

48   "Long before *Jubilee*": "How I Wrote *Jubilee*," HWJ, p. 50.

48   "an awful letter": "Interview with Margaret Walker Alexander," OHP, p. 27.

49   "I felt that": "Interview with Margaret Walker Alexander," OHP, p. 28.

49   "had never seen": "Interview with Margaret Walker Alexander," OHP, p. 29.

49   "I was against": "Interview with Margaret Walker Alexander," OHP, p. 28.

50   "[b]y the time" and "[H]e said": "Interview with Margaret Walker Alexander," OHP, p. 28.

50   "I could not tell": "Interview with Margaret Walker Alexander," OHP, p. 29.

50   "honesty, frankness [and]": "Interview with Margaret Walker Alexander," OHP, p. 29.

51   "I don't think": "Interview with Margaret Walker Alexander," OHP, p. 29.

51   "I would like": UA, p. 10.

51   "awarded grants": "Julius Rosenwald Fund (1917–1948)," ARC, p. 1.

51   "At that time": "How I Wrote *Jubilee*," HWJ, p. 53.

52   "I went into": "How I Wrote *Jubilee*," HWJ, p. 54.

52   "For the first": "How I Wrote *Jubilee*," HWJ, p. 54.

53   "In September 1949": "Black Women in Academia," HWJ, p. 30.

54   "In Greenville": "How I Wrote *Jubilee*," HWJ, p. 55.

55   "[delve] into the": "How I Wrote *Jubilee*," HWJ, p. 56.

55   "the letter Grimes": "How I Wrote *Jubilee*," HWJ, p. 56.

55   "These slave narratives": "How I Wrote *Jubilee*," HWJ, p. 56.

56   "Professor Pearson's": "How I Wrote *Jubilee*," HWJ, p. 57.

56   "[f]rom 1955 until": "How I Wrote *Jubilee*," HWJ, p. 57.

CHAPTER SEVEN

Finishing *Jubilee*: Back to Iowa

57   "People ask me": "How I Wrote *Jubilee*," HWJ, p. 61.

57   "Suddenly all the": "How I Wrote *Jubilee*," HWJ, pp. 57–58.

58   "painful" and "My first short": "How I Wrote *Jubilee*," HWJ, p. 58.

58   "Alma . . .": "How I Wrote *Jubilee*," HWJ, p. 59.

58   "I found myself": "Margaret Walker Alexander," MWT, pp. 142–43.

59   "Kennedy was killed": "Margaret Walker Alexander," MWT, p. 143.

60   "Micah was a": "Micah," PND, p. 27.

60   "Amos is our": "Amos—1963," PND, p. 25.

60   "a man of peace": "Amos (Postscript—1968)," PND, p. 25.

61   "City of tense": "Jackson, Mississippi," PND, pp. 12–13.

62   "Civil War songs": "How I Wrote *Jubilee*," HWJ, p. 60.

62   " . . . I was sick": "How I Wrote *Jubilee*," HWJ, p. 60.

62   "[T]he end of": "How I Wrote *Jubilee*," HWJ, p. 61.

63   "ambitious," "uneven," "fidelity to fact," and "suffered one outrage": PF, p. 2.

63   "even if *Jubilee*": "How I Wrote *Jubilee*," HWJ, p. 50.

63   "one of the": "*Jubilee*," NGE, p. 1.

64   "the slave cabin": "*Jubilee*," NGE, p. 1.

64   "How much of" and "When you have lived": "How I Wrote *Jubilee*," HWJ, p. 62.

64   "The ending of": "*Jubilee*," NGE, p. 2.

CHAPTER EIGHT

Returning Home: Establishing the Institute for the Study of the History, Life, and Culture of Black People

65   "Our greatest weapon": "The Challenge of the 1970s to the Black Scholar," FBF, p. 188.

65   "the royalty checks": "Looking Back: A Conversation with Margaret Walker," MWAT, p. 11.

65, 67   "My southern salesman" and "Black and white": "An Interview with Margaret Walker Alexander," MR, p. 115.

67   "at the forefront": "Mission," MWC, p.1.

67   "Unfortunately Biondi": "The Battle for Black Studies," ITT, p. 1.

68   "controversial issues" and "Not the least": "Critical Approaches to the Study of African American Literature," FBF, pp. 123–124.

68   "dedicated to the": "Brochure," MWC.

69   "Our young people": "Religion, Poetry, and History: Foundations for a New Educational System," FBF, pp. 209, 215.

69   "a major thoroughfare": "Killings at Jackson State," AAR, p. 1.

69   "[w]hen Jackson police": "Mississippi Freedom Trail Marker Commemorates Jackson State Shootings," MDA, p. 1.

70   "Shotguns, high-powered": "Jackson State, May 15, 1970," TMC, pp. 178–179.

70   "painful duty," "expressed the personal," "a number of," and "Your service": "Reflections on May 1970," FBF, pp. 179, 182.

71   "We can be" and "means more than": "Agenda for Action," FBF, pp. 92, 93.

72   "teaching European art" and "a crime against": "Humanities with a Black Focus," FBF, p. 99.

72   "World literature" and "begins with the": "Humanities with a Black Focus," FBF, p. 100.

73   "help[ed] inaugurate": "Chronology," FWB, p. xxiii.

73   "In October of 1972": "Phillis Wheatley and Black Women Writers, 1773–1973," FBF, p. 35.

73   "outstanding black women" and "the first known": "Phillis Wheatley and Black Women Writers, 1773–1973," FBF, pp. 35–36.

73   "Nikki Giovanni": "Phillis Wheatley and Black Women Writers, 1773–1973," FBF, p. 36.

74   "autobiographical and": "Bolder Measures Crashing Through: Margaret Walker's Poem of the Century," FWB, p. 111.

74   "the beginning of a": "Margaret Walker: Black Woman Writer of the South," FWB, p. 46.

75   "I wrote 'October Journey'": "Preface," TMC, p. xv.

76   "Boston is a cold": "Ballad for Phillis Wheatley," TMC, p. 123.

76   "acknowledge[ment of] the": "Phillis Wheatley and Black Women Writers, 1773–1973," FBF, p. 39.

76   "Pretty little black girl": "Ballad for Phillis Wheatley," TMC, p. 123.

CHAPTER NINE

Legal Battles: The Cases against Alex Haley and Ellen Wright

78   "Without *Roots*, I": "Conversation: Margaret Walker Alexander and Joanne V. Gabbin" FF, p. 247.

78   "launched a media": "Remembering Alex Haley and the Roots of His Phenomenal Success," OW, p. 2.

79   "significant parallels": "Preface," FWB, p. xi.

79   "I went through": "An Interview with Margaret Walker Alexander," MR, p. 125.

80   "We went to court": "An Interview with Margaret Walker Alexander," MR, p. 126.

80   "most famous for" and "In his Expert": "Alex Haley and 'Roots': The Lance Armstrong of Literature," BB, p. 1.

80   "I learned all": "Margaret Walker's Reflections and Celebrations: An Interview," TFS, p. 110.

83   "Before he went": "Margaret Walker's Reflections and Celebrations: An Interview," TFS, p. 118.

83   "Highly articulate": "Jesse Jackson, the Man and His Message," FBF, p. 151.

83   "the center of" and "lived with the": "Jesse Jackson, the Man and His Message," FBF, p. 158.

84   "the Jesse Jackson": "Jesse Jackson, the Man and His Message," FBF, p. 160.

84   "When I was asked": "Jesse Jackson, the Man and His Message," FBF, p. 160.

85   "that's the day": "An Interview with Margaret Walker Alexander," MR, p. 123.

85   "I felt Wright": "Margaret Walker," BWW, p. 194.

85   "threefold" and "[T]o define": "Preface," DG, pp. xiv–xv.

85   "permission to quote" and "I view[ed] her request": "Preface," DG, p. xvi.

87   "life as a poet": "Preface," TMC, p. xi.

87   "[a]ll these poems": "Preface," TMC, pp. xvi–xvii.

CHAPTER TEN

Final Years: Awards, Recognitions, and Unfinished Work

88   "She tried to": Margaret Walker Alexander's epitaph

88   "I have compiled": "Preface," HWJ, pp. ix–x.

89   "is not included" and "too few students": "Preface," HWJ, p. ix.

91   "I selected photographs": "A Tribute," MWAT, np.

92   "flawed," "half-written," "not very good," "a number of," and "There are four novels": "A Writer for Her People: An Interview with Dr. Margaret Walker Alexander," MQ, pp. 522–523.

92   "I got three": "Margaret Walker's Reflections and Celebrations: An Interview," TFS, p. 117.

92   "One of the single" and "houses more than": "Mission," MWC website.

93   "three Grande Dames of Mississippi": "University Archives and Museum Receives Rare Portrait of Mississippi Legends," DSU website.

93   "to provide black writers": "Black Literary Hall of Fame Founded," PW, p. 1.

95   "Margaret Walker Alexander": "Margaret Walker Alexander 1916–1998," FMF, p. 1.

95   "She tried to": Margaret Walker Alexander's epitaph.

96   "She was one of": "Margaret Walker Alexander," TN, pp. 1–2.

97   "Margaret Walker remains": "Margaret Walker Alexander," TN, pp. 2–3.

AFTERWORD

The Legacy of Margaret Walker

98   "And when I'm told": "Margaret Walker's Reflections and Celebrations: An Interview," TFS, p. 122.

98   "When I was seventeen": "Margaret Walker's Reflections and Celebrations: An Interview," TFS, p. 122.

99   "adding interviews to": "Civil Rights Documentation Project," JSU, p.1

100   "The manuscript vaults": "History," MWFS, pp. 5–6.

103   "[W]e chose to use": "Conceptual Design Statement," MWFS, p. 18.

103   "features a visual interpretation": "Conceptual Design Statement," MWFS, p. 18.

103   "as a screen tint" and "to stimulate learning": "Conceptual Design Statement,"
       MWFS, p. 18.

103   "'Writer's Connection' gallery": "Conceptual Design Statement," MWFS, p. 18.

APPENDIX 4
Major Adaptations, Recordings, Editions, Dramatic Performances, and Artwork Inspired by Margaret Walker's Work

116   "Dr. Rosia Wade Crisler": "Daughters of Margaret Walker Alexander," DMW, p. 1.

117   "Each of the poem's": LEC, p. 1.

118   "This photo essay": "A Tribute," MWAT, np.

121   *"The Song Cycle* is": CP, np.

121   "This piece was inspired": Cedric Colston, Artist's Note.

121   *"For My People"*: Interview with composer Randy Klein.

Bibliography

—❦—

WORKS BY MARGARET WALKER

For My People. Foreword by Stephen Vincent Benét. Salem, New Hampshire: Ayer Company, Publishers, Inc., 1987.

How I Wrote "Jubilee" and Other Essays on Life and Literature. Ed. Maryemma Graham. New York: The Feminist Press at the City University of New York, 1990.

Jubilee. Boston: Houghton Mifflin, 1966.

On Being Female, Black, and Free: Essays by Margaret Walker, 1932–1992. Ed. Maryemma Graham. Knoxville: University of Tennessee Press, 1997.

Prophets for a New Day. Detroit, Michigan: Broadside Press, 1970.

Richard Wright, Daemonic Genius. New York: Amistad Press, 1988.

This Is My Century: New and Collected Poems. Athens: University of Georgia Press, 1989.

Unpublished Autobiography

OTHER SOURCES

Baraka, Amiri. "Margaret Walker Alexander." *The Nation.* 4 January 1999. http://www.thenation.com/article/margaret-walker-alexander. 1–3.

Barksdale, Richard. "Margaret Walker: Folk Orature and Historical Prophecy." *Black American Poets Between Worlds, 1940–1960.* Knoxville: University of Tennessee Press, 1986. 104–117.

Biondi, Martha. *The Black Revolution on Campus.* Berkeley: University of California Press, 2012.

Bonetti, Kay. "An Interview with Margaret Walker Alexander." *Missouri Review* 15:1 (1992): 11–31.

Campbell, Ruth. "Interview with Margaret Walker." Transcribed from an interview aired on Mississippi Educational Television, August 4, 1983. Reprinted in *Conversations with Margaret Walker,* ed. Maryemma Graham. Jackson: University Press of Mississippi, 2002. 92–97.

Carmichael, Jacqueline Miller. *"Jubilee." The New Georgia Encyclopedia.* http://www.georgi
aencyclopedia.org/nge/ArticlePrintable.jsp?id=h-1242.

———. "Margaret Walker's Reflections and Celebrations: An Interview." *Trumpeting a Fiery Sound: History and Folklore in Margaret Walker's "Jubilee."* Athens: University of Georgia Press, 1998. pp. 103–124.

"Civil Rights Documentation Project." Jackson State University. http://www.usm.edu/crdp/html/jsu.shtml.

Colston, Cedric. *For My People.* Artist's Notes, 2012.

"Composer and Pianist Randy Klein." Margaret Walker Center Press Release. 7 July 2012.

"Conceptual Design Statement." *Margaret Walker Center Feasibility Study.* Margaret Walker Center. August 2013.

Cross, Kim. "Mississippi's Literary Trail." *Southern Living.* http://www.southernliving.com/travel/south-central/mississippi-road-trip-00417000081094/. January 2012.

"Daughters of Margaret Walker Alexander." Press Release. http://www.tulane.edu/~memories/daughters.html.

Freeman, Roland L. "A Tribute." *Margaret Walker's "For My People": A Tribute.* Jackson: University Press of Mississippi, 1992.

Gabbin, Joanne V. "Conversation: Margaret Walker Alexander and Joanne V. Gabbin." *The Furious Flowering of African American Poetry.* Charlottesville: University Press of Virginia, 1999. 239–251.

Gellman, Erik. "National Negro Congress." *Encyclopedia of Chicago.* http://www.encyclopedia.chicagohistory.org/pages/3214.html.

Graham, Maryemma. "I Want to Write, I Want to Write the Songs of My People: The Emergence of Margaret Walker." *Fields Watered with Blood: Critical Essays on Margaret Walker,* ed. Maryemma Graham. Athens: University of Georgia Press, 2001. 11–27.

———. "Chronology." *Fields Watered with Blood: Critical Essays on Margaret Walker,* ed. Maryemma Graham. Athens: University of Georgia Press, 2001. pp. xix–xxvii.

———. "Preface." *Fields Watered with Blood: Critical Essays on Margaret Walker,* ed. Maryemma Graham. Athens: University of Georgia Press, 2001. pp. xi–xiv.

———. "Introduction." *How I Wrote "Jubilee" and Other Essays on Life and Literature,* ed. Maryemma Graham. New York: The Feminist Press at the City University of New York, 1990. pp. xiii–xxi.

Greenlee, Marcia. "Interview with Margaret Walker Alexander." *The Black Women Oral History Project at the Schlesinger Library, Radcliffe College,* ed. Ruth Edmonds Hill. New Providence, NJ: K. G. Saur, 1990. 22 January 1977. 1–64.

Harrison, Alferdteen. "Looking Back: A Conversation with Margaret Walker." In Roland L. Freeman, *Margaret Walker's "For My People": A Tribute.* Jackson: University Press of Mississippi, 1992. 9–12.

Harter, Christopher. "Julius Rosenwald Fund (1917–1948)." Amistad Research Center. http://www.amistadresearchcenter.org/archon/?p=creators/creator&id=154.

Johnson, Hickman M. *Farewell, My Friends! A Book of Eulogies and Tributes.* Bloomington: Trafford Publishing, 2010. 1–5.

Jones, John Griffin. "Margaret Walker Alexander." *Mississippi Writers Talking.* Vol. 2. Jackson: University Press of Mississippi, 1983. 121–146.

Klein, Randy. Interview. 5 September 2013.

Krantz, Rachel, and Elizabeth A. Ryan. "Killings at Jackson State University." *The Biographical Dictionary of Black Americans.* Found at the African American Registry. http://www.aaregistry.org/historic_events/view/killings-jackson-state-university.

Limited Editions Club. *For My People.* http://limitededitionsclub.com/for-my-people/.

Malveaux, Julianne. "The Battle for Black Studies." *In These Times.* 6 October 2012. http://www.inthesetimes.com/article/13814/the_battle_for_black_studies/.

"Margaret Walker: 1915–1998." Poetry Foundation. http://www.poetryfoundation.org/bio/margaret-walker.

Margaret Walker Center Feasibility Study. Margaret Walker Center. August 2013.

Margaret Walker Center Brochure, Margaret Walker Center at Jackson State University.

"Mission." Margaret Walker Center at Jackson State University. http://www.jsums.edu/margaretwalkercenter/42-2/.

"Mississippi Freedom Trail Marker Commemorates Jackson State Shootings." Mississippi Development Authority. 17 April 2012.

Nolte, John. "Alex Haley and 'Roots': The Lance Armstrong of Literature." Breitbart.com. 21 January 2013. http://www.breitbart.com/Big-Journalism/2013/01/21/Alex-Haley-Lance-Armstrong-Of-Literature.

Patrick, Diane. "Black Literary Hall of Fame Founded." *Publishers Weekly.* 15 February 1999. http://www.publishersweekly.com:8080/pw/print/19990215/1854 4-pw-black-literary-hall-of-fame-founded-html. 26 June 2013.

Pettis, Joyce. "Margaret Walker: Black Woman Writer of the South." *Fields Watered with Blood: Critical Essays on Margaret Walker,* ed. Maryemma Graham. Athens: University of Georgia Press, 2001. 44–54.

Reese, Gregg. "Remembering Alex Haley and the Roots of His Phenomenal Success." *Our Weekly.* 11 August 2011. http://www.ourweekly.com/features/remembering-alex-haley-and-roots-his-phenomenal-success. 10 June 2013.

Tate, Claudia. "Margaret Walker." *Black Women Writers at Work.* New York: Continuum, 1983. 188–204.

Traylor, Eleanor. "Bolder Measures Crashing Through: Margaret Walker's Poem of the Century." *Fields Watered with Blood: Critical Essays on Margaret Walker,* ed. Maryemma Graham. Athens: University of Georgia Press, 2001. 110–138.

"University Archives and Museum Receives Rare Portrait of Mississippi Legends." Delta State University. http://www.deltastate.edu/pages/1073.asp?item=5704. 11 September 2009.

Ward, Jerry W., Jr. "A Writer for Her People: An Interview with Dr. Margaret Walker Alexander." *Mississippi Quarterly* 41 (Fall 1988): 515–27.

Wolf, Gillian. "Vivian Gordon Harsh." *Gale Contemporary Black Biography.* Biography from Answers.com. http://www.answers.com/topic/vivian-gordon-harsh.

Credits

ILLUSTRATION CREDITS

Cover photograph of Margaret Walker, also appearing in chapter 5, courtesy of the Harsh Collection at the Chicago Public Library.

Margaret Walker seated alone (in black dress) and with Eudora Welty and Thalia Mara, by permission of photographer H. Kay Holloway.

Margaret Walker's journals, the Jackson State massacre plaque, the Margaret Walker Alexander road sign, the Margaret Walker Alexander branch library, the front entrance of the Margaret Walker Alexander National Research Center, the exhibit area and gift shop inside the center, and the image of children playing by artist Elizabeth Catlett from the Limited Editions Club's *For My People*, photographs courtesy of Red Squared Productions.

Langston Hughes at the University of North Carolina–Chapel Hill, courtesy of Louis Round Wilson Special Collections Library, the University of North Carolina at Chapel Hill.

Central Building, Haven Institute, and Brainerd Hall, Central Alabama Institute, from an electronic edition of *Methodist Adventures in Negro Education* (1922) from the North Carolina Collection, Wilson Special Collections Library, the University of North Carolina at Chapel Hill.

The Sundown Sign, courtesy of the Collection of the Tubman African American Museum, Macon, Georgia.

The main card catalog, reading room, and exterior of Deering Library at Northwestern University and Margaret Walker's application for admission to Northwestern, courtesy of Northwestern University Archives.

Richard Wright, and the Women's Reading Group, Hall Branch, Chicago Public Library, courtesy of the Harsh Collection at the Chicago Public Library.

W. E. B. Du Bois, Billie Holiday, Jesse Jackson, and the 1939 World's Fair, courtesy of the Library of Congress, Prints and Photographs Division.

The bus showing the separation of blacks and whites, courtesy of Birmingham, Alabama, Public Library Archives.

Paul Engle, courtesy of Frederick W. Kent Collection, University of Iowa Libraries, Iowa City, Iowa.

Thesis cover page: Walker, Margaret. "For My People; A Volume of Verse." M.A. thesis, University of Iowa, 1940. 50 pp.

Stephen Vincent Benét from the Yale College 1919 yearbook, courtesy of Manuscripts and Archives, Yale University.

Margaret Walker with Elizabeth Catlett's bust of Phillis Wheatley, Margaret Walker (pointing), Nikki Giovanni and Tougaloo College gospel choir, and Phillis Wheatley Poetry Festival participants, by permission of Roy Lewis Photography.

Margaret Walker with her grandchildren; Margaret Walker and Roland L. Freeman (2-65782/25); Margaret Walker's body lying in state (4-84979/13); Margaret Walker with Dr. Alferdteen Harrison (3-920008/34); Margaret Walker at the reception following the opening of the opera *Jubilee* (24-15774/6 and 24-15774/25); Margaret Walker reading poetry with family and friends (10-92005/12); Margaret Walker at the Margaret Walker Alexander National Research Center (48088/8); and Margaret Walker and Jerry W. Ward, Jr. (3-65871/14), by permission of Roland L. Freeman. Photographs © 2013 Roland L. Freeman.

Margaret Walker with Dr. Maryemma Graham, by permission of David Rae Morris. Photograph © David Rae Morris.

Firnist and Margaret Walker Alexander's grave marker, by permission of Carla Wall.

"For the boys and girls who grew up in spite of these things . . ." from *For My People*, the Limited Editions Club, 1992, and *For My People—With Love, for Margaret, My Friend*, 1987 by Elizabeth Catlett, Art © Catlett Mora Family Trust/Licensed by VAGA, New York, NY.

The performance of *For My People: The Margaret Walker Song Cycle*, courtesy of Randy Klein and Charise Lewis Photography.

Artwork by Cedric Colston, by permission of Cedric Colston, photograph courtesy of Red Squared Productions.

Margaret Walker at Square Books in Oxford, Mississippi, and at the Beinecke Collection at Yale University, New Haven, Connecticut, courtesy of the William R. Ferris Collection, Southern Folklife Collection, Wilson Library, University of North Carolina at Chapel Hill.

Guynes Street Garden Club, by permission of Myrlie Evers.

Margaret Walker speaking at Port Gibson High School's graduation ceremony, by permission of Patricia Crosby.

Margaret Walker photographed by Carl Van Vechten, courtesy of the Yale Collection of American Literature, Beinecke Rare Book and Manuscript Library. Published with permission of the Van Vechten Trust.

Illustrations on the following pages are reprinted courtesy of the Margaret Walker Center, Jackson State University: 4, 5, 6, 7, 16, 50, 53, 54, 59, 63, 66, 67, 72, 74, 75, 79, 80, 81, 84, 91, 93, 100, 122 (bottom), 124

Illustrations on the following pages are reprinted courtesy of Will W. Alexander Library, Dillard University: 7, 14, 15, 16, 17

Illustratios on the following pages are reprinted courtesy of Charlotte Moman: 56, 82, 87 (left), 90 (top), 112, 114, 123 (bottom left)

Index

Page numbers in **boldface** indicate an illustration.